LEGENDS OF FLIGHT

S.E. 210
CARAVELLE

A Legends of Flight Illustrated History

WOLFGANG BORGMANN

SCHIFFER MILITARY

4880 Lower Valley Road • Atglen, PA 19310

Dedication
To my father, Harald Borgmann, who was closely associated with the
Caravelle over a long period of his professional life.

Other Schiffer books by the author
*McDonnell Douglas DC-10/MD-11: A Legends of Flight Illustrated
    History*, 978-0-7643-6137-1
Boeing 707: A Legends of Flight Illustrated History, 978-0-7643-6345-0
Boeing 737: A Legends of Flight Illustrated History, 978-0-7643-6138-8

Other Schiffer books on related subjects
Boeing 757: A Legends of Flight Illustrated History,
    Dan Dornseif, 978-0-7643-6346-7

Translated from the German by David Johnston

Library of Congress Control Number: 2022944556

Designed by Christopher Bower
Cover design by Molly Shields
Type set in DIN Alternate/Minion Pro

ISBN: 978-0-7643-6650-5
Printed in India

Published by Schiffer Publishing, Ltd.
4880 Lower Valley Road
Atglen, PA 19310
Phone: (610) 593-1777; Fax: (610) 593-2002
Email: Info@schifferbooks.com
Web: www.schifferbooks.com

For our complete selection of fine books on this and related subjects,
please visit our website at www.schifferbooks.com. You may also
write for a free catalog.

Schiffer Publishing's titles are available at special discounts for
bulk purchases for sales promotions or premiums. Special editions,
including personalized covers, corporate imprints, and excerpts, can
be created in large quantities for special needs. For more information,
contact the publisher.

We are always looking for people to write books on new and
related subjects. If you have an idea for a book, please contact us at
proposals@schifferbooks.com.

CONTENTS

Among other things, Helsinki Airport was home to the Finnair Caravelle 10B3 fleet. Here, Super Caravelle OH-LSH attracts the attention of passengers waiting for it to depart in 1973. *Courtesy of Finnish Aviation Museum*

INTRODUCTION

The ability to cover long distances as quickly as possible was one of the outstanding characteristics of the Portuguese and Spanish caravela ships with which the traditional seafaring nations set out to establish new trade routes around the globe in the fifteenth century. Vasco da Gama, for example, explored the sea route from Europe to India with three caravela in 1498–1499, while Christopher Columbus discovered America with the legendary Niña and Pinta in 1492. Looking for a suitable name for their new jet, which was also intended to open up new, fast trade routes, the French aircraft makers found their inspiration in precisely those historical sailing-ship models. Translated from the Portuguese caravela into French, it became the Caravelle.

If the old aviation adage "If it looks good, it flies good" ever applied to an aircraft type, then it certainly applies to the S.E. 210. But not only is it elegant, above all it impresses with technical innovation. It was the first jet to have two tail-mounted engines, a flight control system operated exclusively by hydraulic pressure, without control cables, and many other technological innovations that delighted airline managers, technicians, and pilots around the world. On December 28, 1968, for example, it became the first passenger jet to be certified for blind landings in poor visibility in Category III conditions (horizontal visibility: 500 ft. / decision height: 50 ft.). Its good flight characteristics were legendary, with a glide ratio of around 20, which corresponds to the performance profile of early gliders. This means that for every 3.3 feet (1 meter) of altitude, the Caravelle could fly 65.6 feet (20 meters) even in poor meteorological conditions! There are two record-breaking glides by passenger jets, each from an altitude of around 39,370 feet (12 kilometers), with the engines idling. On one flight the aircraft covered 165 miles (265 kilometers)—on the other, 203 miles (327 kilometers)—directly to the landing approaches of their respective destinations. The passengers, on the other hand, appreciated the quiet passenger cabin and the supersoft landings made possible by the optimized landing gear. The teardrop-shaped cabin windows so typical of the Caravelle also offered an excellent view of the cloud formations—and the world below.

This friendly crew of an ALIA Caravelle 10R invites you to fly through the fascinating history of the S.E. 210. *Courtesy of Royal Jordanian Airlines*

Author Wolfgang Borgmann was invited on May 24, 1980, to join the cockpit crew of an Air France Caravelle III for the one-hour-and-one- minute-long flight from Stuttgart to Paris CDG. *Author's collection*

The *caravela* ship types that carried the legendary Portuguese and Spanish explorers of the fifteenth century gave the Caravelle its name. The Portuguese airline TAP Air Portugal, however, used the original name Caravela on its S.E. 210 VI-R. *Courtesy of Tom Weihe*

There are phone calls that stay with one forever. Like the call in October 2010 that began with the words "Mr. Borgmann, would you like to buy a Caravelle for one Euro?" What I initially thought was a bad joke quickly turned out to be a very serious question from a colleague who knew about my enthusiasm for old aircraft. After all, it was the first Caravelle production aircraft with the construction number 1—which had served with Air France with the registration F-BHRA and the aircraft name Alsace—and was now threatened with scrapping. Completely preserved, in almost perfect condition, it was at the Centre d'instruction de Vilgénis, the Air France training center near Paris-Orly airport, and was soon to make way for more-modern training aids for future aviation technicians. "Just one euro"—this seductive message made me start dreaming. But in the end, common sense prevailed, or rather the realization that the costs associated with dismantling and transporting such a large object from the French capital to Germany were beyond the realms of possibility for me personally, and for the exhibition venues I had requested in museums and airfields. And so today this Caravelle sits in a small Dutch aviation museum, even if after many years out of doors it is no longer as perfectly preserved as it was back then in the big hangar at Vilgénis.

Not only did the Caravelle's large, teardrop-shaped windows give passengers a good view of the outside, but they also optimally distributed the forces acting on the airframe, thus avoiding overloading, cracking, and structural failure like that which plagued the earlier de Havilland Comet. *Courtesy of www.aviationancestry.co.uk*

Sud-Aviation offered the version 10A equipped with General Electric "aft fan" engines exclusively as the Super Caravelle or Horizon after the French manufacturer parted ways with its US partner Douglas. *Courtesy of www. aviationancestry.co.uk*

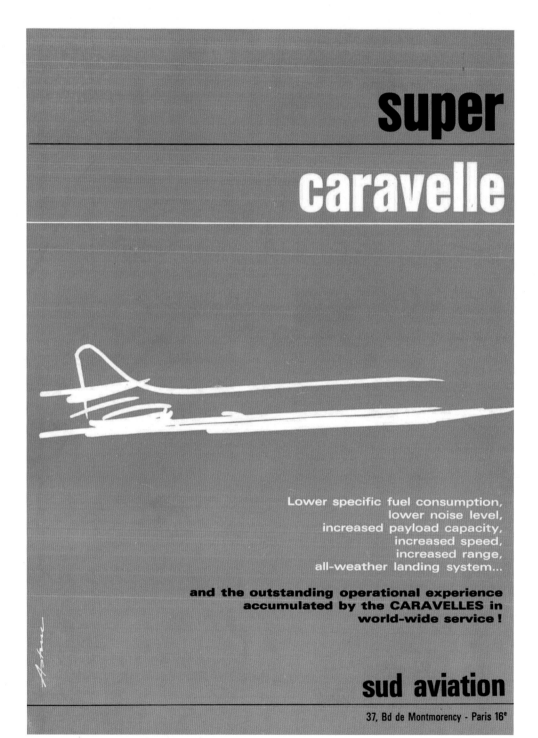

super

caravelle

Lower specific fuel consumption, lower noise level, increased payload capacity, increased speed, increased range, all-weather landing system...

and the outstanding operational experience accumulated by the CARAVELLES in world-wide service !

sud aviation

37, Bd de Montmorency - Paris 16ᵉ

In 1980, I was privileged to fly for the first time as a passenger on board one of these revolutionary—although at that time already old—jets. I got to know and love the original Caravelle III and the stretched Super 12. At the beginning of the 1980s, their elegant, soft silhouette and the distinctive teardrop-shaped passenger windows were already an anachronism compared to other modern jets of that era. Nevertheless, it was not until the 1990s that the last aircraft gradually disappeared from the skies over Europe, having already made their final rounds on other continents. The last aircraft in regular passenger service even survived into the next millennium and was taken out of service by Waltair, based in the Democratic Republic of Congo, only in 2005. So this book is my own personal declaration of love to a beautiful French woman with European genes. After all, there is much more Europe in her than the engineering of the Sud-Est design team would suggest. Born in Toulouse in the South of France, the current headquarters of Airbus and the regional aircraft manufacturer ATR, she was the beginning of European cooperation in aircraft design and construction.

The S.E. 210 Caravelle III Alsace, which was offered to the author of this book for one Euro, in the Air France training hangar at Vilgénis. This was the first production aircraft with construction number 1! *Author's collection*

There's music in the air. The story of the SAS "Caravelle Samba," recorded by the Cliff Adams Singers in 1959 as a musical homage by Scandinavian Airlines to its S.E. 210s, and many other exciting Caravelle stories are part of this book, which I hope you enjoy reading.

Wolfgang Borgmann
Oerlinghausen, Germany
Autumn 2022

Author Wolfgang Borgmann at the controls of the Caravelle simulator at the renowned pilot-training center TFC European Airline Services GmbH in the city of Essen in the German Ruhr region. *Courtesy of Christian Käufer, www.tfc-kaeufer.de*

CHAPTER 1
THE BEGINNING OF THE JET AGE

A Caravelle of the Brazilian airline Panair do Brasil flying over Rio de Janeiro in the 1960s. The Botafogo district in the foreground not only has an excellent view of the striking Sugar Loaf but will also be familiar to accomplished samba dancers—after all, it is the namesake of a particularly impressive dance step. *Courtesy of Ministério da Defesa / Comando da Aeronáutica / Museu Aeroespacial, Rio de Janeiro*

There was something in the air—this is how one could describe the development of the jet engine. In parallel, and ignorant of the other's work, German designer Joachim Pabst von Ohain and his British counterpart Frank Whittle developed the first jet engines, which were launched on August 27, 1939, during the maiden flight of the German Heinkel He 178 V1 experimental aircraft, and two years later by a British Gloster E.28/39. Following the military jets, the jet age in civil aviation began at the end of the 1940s. The Vickers 618 Nene Viking, an experimental aircraft, became world famous when it flew from London Heathrow to the military airfield at Paris-Villacoublay in thirty-four minutes and seven seconds on April 6, 1948, with twenty-four passengers on board. This was the world premiere of a pure jetliner, albeit only an experimental one! Not only did it halve the usual flying time of a propeller-driven aircraft, it also achieved this feat on the thirty-ninth anniversary of the first crossing of the English Channel between France and Great Britain by Louis Blériot. Number two in the jet sky was the Avro 688 Tudor 8, a flying research laboratory. Like the modified Vickers Viking, it was powered by Rolls-Royce Nene engines. Four of these were required to power the only Tudor 8 to be built, when it made its first

This Panair do Brasil Caravelle VI-R displays its large wing area during a turn to port over the Brazilian coast. The aerodynamic design of the Caravelle's wings made it an excellent glider, with a performance comparable to sailplanes. *Courtesy of Ministério da Defesa / Comando da Aeronáutica / Museu Aeroespacial, Rio de Janeiro*

flight from the Avro factory airfield in Woodford, England, on September 6, 1948. Its primary task was to investigate the behavior of the new Rolls-Royce engines at high altitudes.

Next in the line of early jetliners was the de Havilland 106 Comet. On July 27, 1949, the prototype Comet G-5-1 (G-ALVG) took off on its maiden flight from Hatfield, United Kingdom, with chief pilot John Cunningham at the controls. The second prototype, with the registration G-5-2 (G-ALZK), followed one year later. It immediately joined the extensive flight test program, which had its finale with certification by the British aviation authority on January 22, 1952. At 1512 on the afternoon of May 2, 1952, BOAC ceremoniously opened the jet age. On that day, Comet 1, registration G-ALYP, took off from London Airport on the first scheduled jet flight in aviation history. After five refueling stops, it arrived at Johannesburg, South Africa, in twenty-three hours and thirty-seven minutes. The smooth flight made possible by the new jet engines delighted the Comet passengers of the first hour. But the enthusiasm came to a tragic end with the crash of BOAC Comet 1 G-ALYP on January 10, 1954, and its sister aircraft G-ALYY on April 8, 1954. The most extensive accident investigation in aviation history to date revealed that metal fatigue had led to the structural failure of both Comet fuselages—with fatal consequences for passengers and crews. The de Havilland engineers had ventured so far into new technological territory with the D.H. 106 Comet that they

The Vickers Nene Viking was a converted Viking propeller-driven aircraft. Although it was the first passenger aircraft with pure jet propulsion, just a single prototype was built. When testing had been completed, it was converted back into a propeller aircraft with piston engines. *Courtesy of www.aviationancestry.co.uk*

ACHIEVEMENT

The Vickers "Nene/Viking"

Powered by Rolls-Royce

the first all-jet airliner in the world to fly

ENGINES

ROLLS-ROYCE LIMITED DERBY

JET-PROPELLED LABORATORY

Britain's first four engined jet-propelled air liner, the Avro Tudor VIII with Rolls-Royce Nene engines will give Avro engineers first hand experience in solving some of the operational problems of the aircraft of the future. The benefit of this intensive and prolonged research will, of course, be passed on to the air line operator.

TUDOR VIII

A. V. ROE & CO. LTD. AVRO MANCHESTER
BRANCH OF THE HAWKER SIDDELEY GROUP

could not have foreseen the dangers. In order to prevent similar disasters, the British authorities made the investigation report public with all the technical details, which allowed the tragically gained knowledge to flow directly into the designs of the Sud-Est 210 Caravelle, which was already under development, but also of the American long-range jets, the Boeing 707 and Douglas DC-8. Since then, all commercial aircraft have been built according to the so-called "fail-safe" principle. This philosophy of fail-safe construction states that the failure of a single component must not lead to the failure of the entire system. Rather, another component must be able to take over its function until the next routine check at the latest. To prevent catastrophes, crack stoppers ensure that damage cannot spread uncontrollably through the structure and lead to its failure. Again and again, we read that the nose section of the Caravelle was taken directly from the Comet 1. This is true of its basic design and especially the layout of the pilot's cockpit with instruments, thrust levers, and control columns, which were partly adopted 1:1 from the D.H. 106. The nose structure, however, was redesigned, reinforced, and made "fail safe" as a result of the Comet crashes.

Like the Nene Viking, the Avro Tudor VIII was an experimental jet converted from a propeller-driven airliner. It was used primarily to investigate the high-altitude behavior of the jet engines then under development. *Courtesy of www.aviationancestry.co.uk*

On May 2, 1952, a de Havilland Comet of the British airline BOAC inaugurated the jet age of air travel with the first scheduled flight by a passenger jet.

Final assembly of the first S.E. 210 Caravelle III production aircraft for SAS at Sud-Aviation in Toulouse. *Courtesy of SAS Museum*

AVRO CANADA JETLINER: THE UNLUCKY CONTENDER

It wasn't the British Avro 706 Ashton experimental aircraft, which flew before the Caravelle, or the further developed de Havilland 106 Comet 2 and 3, or the four-engine Boeing Dash 80, but the Canadian Avro Canada C-102 Jetliner that could have become a serious competitor for the Caravelle—had it gone into production!

In contrast to the early British jet test beds, which were based on existing piston-engine types, the Canadian Jetliner with its four Rolls-Royce Derwent Type 5/17 engines was a completely new design. Conceived to carry thirty-six passengers, the C-102 first took to the skies on August 10, 1949, just thirteen days after the de Havilland 106 Comet. The prototype of the passenger aircraft designed by Canadian aerospace engineer J. C. "Jim" Floyd was sent on extensive sales tours throughout the United States, where it met with great interest among the airlines, but also from the US Air Force for use as a liaison aircraft. National Airlines was ready to order the aircraft as the launch customer, while American Airlines, Eastern Airlines, and United were waiting for the go-ahead for series production. The C-102 had a special fan in the American aviation tycoon Howard Hughes. Together with the managers of Trans World Airlines (TWA), which he controlled, he predicted a bright future for this jet type. Howard Hughes even planned to produce the C-102 under license in the United States through his Hughes Aircraft Company, in cooperation with Convair. The enthusiasm was justified, because the Jetliner was able to fly faster, higher, quieter, farther, and more economically than any propeller aircraft operated domestically by TWA at that time! On April 8–9, 1952, Howard Hughes had the opportunity to inspect the four-engine jet close-up at the airport of his Californian residence, Culver City, outside Los Angeles and to take the controls during a test flight. Negotiations among Hughes, Convair, and Avro Canada on the planned start of production dragged on for several months, until the outbreak of the Korean War brought the entire C-102 program to an abrupt end. Both Canada and the United States were involved in the fighting and prohibited the use of Avro Canada and Hughes capacity for the production of a commercial aircraft, since these were now needed for military projects. Thus, after its final flight on November 23, 1956, the only example of a Jetliner to be built, with the registration CF-EJD-X, was scrapped. Only the nose section survived, and it is preserved in the Canadian Aviation Museum in Ottawa—and this hopeful project was discontinued for all time.

Although the nose sections of the de Havilland 106 Comet and the S.E. 210 appear to be identical, Sud-Aviation modified their design into a "fail-safe" construction. This was a consequence of the series of crashes involving the Comet 1 that were caused by fatigue. *Author photograph (top), Thai Airways International (right)*

The Avro Canada C-102 Jetliner would have had a good chance to succeed on the world market. However, after their countries entered the Korean War, Canadian and American aircraft manufacturers were forced to switch production completely to military aircraft. So only one prototype was built. *Courtesy of Avro Canada*

CHAPTER 2
THE S.E. 210: A WINNING DESIGN CONCEPT

One of the two Caravelle prototypes in flight over the city center of Toulouse. After the Caravelle, the southern French metropolis was the center of production for the French share of the Concorde supersonic jet. Since the late 1960s, however, the focus has been on the production of the aircraft of the European Airbus consortium and the ATR turboprops. *Courtesy of Ministério da Defesa / Comando da Aeronáutica / Museu Aeroespacial, Rio de Janeiro*

In 1955, the S.E. 210 Caravelle, a technologically revolutionary jetliner, took off from Toulouse on its maiden flight. With this first successful Western-built jetliner, the French manufacturer Sud-Aviation laid the foundation for today's short- and medium-haul jet air transport sector. When the French government and airline body Comité du Matériel Civil voted in favor of the national project for a short- and medium-range jet on October 12, 1951, on the other side of the English Channel the British de Havilland Aircraft Company was in the middle of the test program for its D.H. 106 Comet. This first series-produced, jet-powered commercial aircraft received its British type certificate on January 22, 1952. In contrast to the French plans, however, the first production version of the Comet was designed for long-haul routes. Shorter distances, according to the unanimous opinion of most manufacturers and airlines, would in the long run be reserved for more-economical aircraft with piston or turboprop engines, such as the Vickers Viscount. They were to be mistaken! Regardless of all these concerns, the French aircraft manufacturers Bréguet / SNCA du Nord, Hurel-Dubois, SNCA du Sud-Ouest, and SNCA du Sud-Est worked feverishly on the jet designs they hoped would emerge victorious from the national development program. The Sud-Est team, led by Pierre Satre, finally prevailed over its competitors with its X-210 project. Initially conceived as a three-engine aircraft powered by French SNECMA Atar E3 engines, Sud-Est changed their X-210 to a twin-engine version with more-powerful Rolls-Royce R.A. 16 Avon engines at the request of the selection committee. This concept was submitted to the French Secretariat of Civil Aviation (SGACC) for review in July 1952. The design seemed to have convinced right away, because just two months later, the Société Nationale de Construction Aéronautique du Sud-Est Aviation (SNCASE), Sud-Est Aviation for short, named the winner. On January 3, 1953, a contract for the construction of two flying prototypes as well as one fuselage each for material fatigue tests in a water tank and for static tests was signed between SNCASE and the French state, which also assumed the costs—and work began just one month later. Even before the final confirmation of the order by the SGACC on July 6, 1953, the project lost its X experimental status and from then on was officially called S.E. 210.

Like the later Airbus project, the Caravelle was also a product of international cooperative partners—even if the French share predominated. The forward fuselage section, including the cockpit, was preassembled at the Marseille-Marignane plant; the plant in Nantes, Brittany, was responsible for wing production; the Saint-Nazaire and Rochefort plants were involved in the production of the tail unit as well as the landing flaps and leading edges of the wings; and two plants in the Paris area supplied cabin components, while the Toulouse plant was responsible for the fuselage and final assembly as well as flight testing. International partners Fiat of Italy produced the engine nacelles, aileron, and tail components; the US company Lockheed, in its British factory, the servo system for the flight controls; and other American companies produced the autopilot, electronic components, and air-conditioning for the passenger cabin, among other things. As engine suppliers, the British Rolls-Royce works and, in the course of the project, Pratt & Whitney in the United States also had a significant share in the total value of each aircraft.

Before the British Comet was withdrawn from service in the spring of 1954 as a result of a series of crashes, SNCASE planned to cooperate closely with de Havilland to offer both types to the airlines as part of a family concept—the four-engine Comet for long-haul and the twin-engine S.E. 210 for medium-haul routes. This is the reason why the Caravelle uses imperial measurements and why the nose sections of both types, including the cockpit layout, look confusingly similar. This concept was of particular interest to Air France and the equally French UAT but came to nothing because of the sudden grounding of the British jetliner. The Caravelle owed its later sales success in particular to the economy and reliability of its engines, which were satisfactory by the standards of the time. After the versions I to VI-R were equipped with British Rolls-Royce Avon engines, Sud-Aviation chose the American Pratt & Whitney JT8D as the standard engine for all further developments—up to the final version the Caravelle 12 "Super Douze" (Super Twelve). After the first jet engines with centrifugal-flow compressors, such as the de Havilland Ghost and Rolls-Royce Nene, the Avon was the first British engine to be produced in quantity with the axial compressor design that is still used today to power military and civil aircraft. Various compressor stages are arranged one behind the other on the central axis, which enables much-simpler construction and higher performance compared to engines designed with centrifugal compressors. The Avon was one of the most successful early jet engines, with over 11,000 units produced. In the civil sector, it was the exclusive power plant for the four-engine de Havilland Comet 2, 3, 4, and 4C versions, in addition to the twin-engine Caravelle. To this day, it is used as an industrial gas turbine; for example, as a pump in offshore gas and oil production, or as an emergency generator in power plants around the globe. However, this type of engine was mainly used to power twelve British, Swedish, and American military aircraft. These included the Vickers Valiant and English Electric Canberra bombers as well as the Hawker Hunter and Saab 35 Draken fighter aircraft, to name but a few. The French proved to be just as lucky in their choice of engine type for the more advanced Caravelle 10 to 12, which featured a higher takeoff weight and greater range.

After a brief interlude, which included a proposal to install the General Electric CJ805-23C "aft fan" engine as part of an offer to the former US airline TWA, the final choice fell on the Pratt & Whitney JT8D. It would become the standard power plant for the twin- and three-engine jets of the 1960s, 1970s, and even 1980s. This engine was not only more powerful than the Rolls-Royce Avon, but also more economical and, above all, considerably quieter due to its turbofan design. However, the JT8D-1, -7, and -9 versions installed in the Caravelle could not really be called "quiet" in the sense of a modern commercial aircraft of the twenty-first century. For the airlines, the choice of the JT8D also brought potential synergies if their fleets included other aircraft powered by this engine—for example, the Boeing 727 and 737, the Douglas DC-9, or the Dassault Mercure. The latter was used exclusively by the French domestic airline Air Inter but was operated there in parallel with the Caravelle 12 with the same American fan engines on domestic routes.

The design of the Caravelle was akin to a technical revolution in aircraft construction. This design, later emulated by the BAC-111, Douglas DC-9,

A rare color photo of the Caravelle final-assembly hangar. Construction number 172, intended for SAS, was delivered to the Scandinavian airline on December 17, 1964, with the registration SE-DAC, and was christened Dag Viking. *Courtesy of Finnish Aviation Museum*

Fokker F28, and Tupolev Tu 134, limited the noise in the passenger cabin to the rear rows of seats. This made a trip aboard the S.E. 210 a very pleasant experience for most passengers. No wonder the Caravelle was highly favored by air travelers still accustomed to the vibration and noise of propeller-driven aircraft with piston engines in the 1950s and 1960s. Those living near airports, on the other hand, were less pleased with this technical progress, which was accompanied by an infernal noise from the two Rolls-Royce Avon engines. Even Hamburg Air, the Hamburg Airport magazine at the time, commented critically on the first landing by the Caravelle prototype in the Hanseatic city: "We were thrilled by the sleekness of the machine, its comfort, its short takeoff distance, and its speed. We were not at all thrilled by the noise during takeoff. However, technicians, politicians, and experts were unanimous in their opinion that the last word had not yet been said about this. The designers' constant efforts to reduce noise levels, even at the expense of engine performance, will surely lead to an acceptable decibel level by the time the plane enters service." Unfortunately, the editors were wrong!

Meeting of two generations of air transport at Copenhagen Airport. In the foreground, the second Caravelle prototype, with the registration F-BHHI. Behind it, the SAS Douglas DC-6 Alf Viking, with piston engine propulsion. *Courtesy of SAS*

The Caravelle prototype F-BHHI was shown not only to SAS in Copenhagen, but also to Finnair in Helsinki on February 7, 1958. The two cross-country skiers on the apron, as interested spectators, prove that security measures at airports were not as strict back then as they are today. *Courtesy of Finnish Aviation Museum*

DEVELOPMENT: FROM SERIES I TO SUPER DOUZE

The first flights by the two prototypes 01 and 02, with the registrations F-WHHH and F-WHHI, on May 25, 1955, and May 6, 1956, were followed by an extensive flight test program, which culminated in certification by the French aviation authority on April 2, 1958—followed by the American FAA approval six days later. The flight debut of the first production model, the Caravelle I, took place on May 18 of that year. The production version, which was 4.9 feet (1.5 meters) longer than the prototypes, had more-powerful Rolls-Royce R.A. 29 Avon engines. Its most distinctive feature, however, was the HF antenna on the roof of the passenger cabin, resulting in a long dorsal fin that merged directly into the vertical stabilizer. Higher takeoff weights and cruising speeds characterized the Caravelle IA and III versions offered from 1960 onward, with further improved Rolls-Royce Avon R.A.29/1 Mk. 526 and R.A.29/3 Mk. 527 engines. The Caravelle VI-N, powered by two Rolls-Royce Avon Mk. 531 engines, followed just one year later.

Stewardesses of Scandinavian Airlines pose under an engine nacelle of the Caravelle prototype during its visit to Stockholm-Bromma airport. In those days the city airport of the Swedish capital was home to the SAS head office. *SAS Museum*

Rolls-Royce chose an Avro Lancastrian as the flying test bed for its Nene engines. For safety reasons, it retained the two inboard Rolls-Royce Merlin engines, and only the two outboard engines were replaced by Nene jet engines. *Courtesy of www.aviationancestry.co.uk*

Rolls-Royce Avon engine change on an Austrian Airlines Caravelle VI-R in 1968. The aircraft, registration OE-LCU, was originally a build number reserved for TWA's order of twenty Caravelle 10As. *Courtesy of Austrian Airlines*

Tail view of a SAS SE 210 III with the characteristic slim engine nacelles, covering the original Rolls-Royce Avon engines. *Norwegian Technical Museum*

On February 10, 1960, the US aircraft maker Douglas Aircraft Company signed a far-reaching cooperation agreement with Sud-Aviation. The agreement stipulated that Douglas would be responsible for sales and technical support for all customers, with the exception of airlines based in Europe and the French-speaking regions around the globe. Should the monthly Caravelle production rate exceed eight aircraft, it was also planned to establish a second final-assembly line at Douglas's Long Beach plant in California. As an outward sign of the cooperation, the Caravelle III with the factory registration F-WJAM received a "Douglas Sud Aviation" hybrid livery and henceforth served as a demonstrator stationed in the United States, with the US registration N420GE and the aircraft name Santa Maria. It was this aircraft that was sent on sales tours around the world as the Caravelle 10A, powered by General Electric CJ805-23C engines. Two weeks after the signing of the agreement, on February 25, 1960, United Airlines ordered twenty Caravelle VI-Rs supplemented by options for twenty more. This was the first version of the S.E. 210 to have thrust reversers. These eliminated the need for the braking chute, required by the first Caravelles for landings on short and wet or icy runways. Following a requirement by the US Federal Aviation Administration (FAA), the aircraft destined for United received larger cockpit windows for the first time, giving the pilots a better all-around view. Further modifications included improved aerodynamics of the wings. Sud Aviation hoped for a breakthrough in the US market after the order for twenty Caravelle 10As by Trans World Airlines Inc. General Electric had taken delivery of N420GE in July 1960 as a test aircraft for the new engine. From then on, the Santa Maria went in search of customers with two of these CJ805-23C "aft fans," in which the large fan was mounted behind the combustion chamber, rotating freely in the jet stream. But these dreams were shattered only two years later, when TWA canceled its order for economic reasons. The relationship between Sud-Aviation and Douglas cooled dramatically and was ended by mutual agreement shortly afterward, when Douglas began design work on its own twin-engine short-and-medium-haul jet,

Final preparations for a night flight by a Caravelle III of SAS on the apron at Copenhagen Airport. *Courtesy of SAS Museum*

The Colombian airline Aerotal acquired this Caravelle VI-R with the registration HK-1780 and the construction number 160 from Lan Chile in August 1975. The latter had received the Caravelle new from Sud-Aviation with the registration CC-CCQ on July 2 of the previous year. This photo was taken in March 1980 at Bogotá El Dorado International Airport. *Courtesy of AirNikon Collection, Pima Air and Space Museum*

the Model 2086, in October 1961, which gave rise to the DC-9. In addition to numerous technological advances, the Douglas jet had a great advantage over the Caravelle in that it could be flown in the United States by two pilots instead of three. This was due to the fact that the maximum takeoff weight of the Caravelle, in contrast to the DC-9, was above the magic limit set by the American FAA, which required a minimum crew of three men—or women—in the cockpit.

After this transatlantic parting of the ways, Sud-Aviation offered the 10A version, now called the Horizon or Super Caravelle, with "aft fan" engines but without its former American partner. But no customers could be found for it, even under French ownership. More successful was the S.E. 210 10B, with Pratt & Whitney JT8D engines, which were the industry standard at the time, as described above.

For the first time, the rows of windows were raised by 20 centimeters to improve the outside view for the passengers. In the nomenclature, the 10B3 variant, for which Finnair placed the first order—followed by the Danish charter airline Sterling—stood out for several reasons. It was 3 feet, 3 inches longer than the 10B, had a higher maximum takeoff weight, and could carry a maximum of 104 passengers, instead of ninety-nine. The Caravelle 10B and 10R models, with more-powerful JT8D-7 engines, and the 11R combi version eventually paved the way for the ultimate Caravelle. The Danish charter airline Sterling was the launch customer for the Super 12, whose fuselage was stretched by almost 14 feet compared to the base model.

Powered by two JT8D-9 engines, the Caravelle 12 could accommodate up to 140 passengers in charter-seating configuration. After the delivery of five more Super Douze

Sud-Aviation and Douglas also sent N420GE, modified with General Electric "aft fan" engines, to Helsinki in 1961. The hope was to convince Finnair to buy this more advanced version. Here the slender engine core and the shrouded fan behind it are clearly visible. *Courtesy of Finnish Aviation Museum*

(Super Twelves) to the French domestic airline Air Inter, production of the S.E. 210 Caravelle ended in 1973 after a total of 282 aircraft had been built. By then, the manufacturer was no longer called Sud-Aviation but had merged with the likewise state-owned aviation companies Nord Aviation and Société d'étude et de réalisation d'engins balistiques (SÉREB) to form Société Nationale Industrielle Aérospatiale (SNIAS), which was in the midst of preparations for series production of the Airbus A300B in Toulouse!

This excerpt from the Sud-Aviation S.E. 210 Instruction Manual of July 1, 1958, describes the basic thoughts of the Caravelle design team on the design of the jet—especially the aspect of fatigue. This was the factor that had led to the crash of two de Havilland Comet 1s just four years earlier and thus to the premature end of the first attempt at regular scheduled jet flights. The following is from the original English translation prepared for Sud Aviation and has been left in its original form despite its, at times, stilted language:

This in-flight photo impressively demonstrates the unusual appearance of the "aft fans" installed on the Caravelle. Modern fan engines have the fan in the front—these General Electric engines, however, have a fan in the rear, rotating freely in the engine exhaust stream. *Courtesy of Finnish Aviation Museum*

After the end of its cooperative arrangement with Douglas, Sud-Aviation tried to sell the Caravelle equipped with the GE "aft fans" on its own. However, not a single customer was found. *Courtesy of www.aviationancestry.co.uk*

An aircraft is designed according to a specific program which is drawn up by an executive authority or by potential users. The outcome of this program is a project which is modified progressively in accordance with discussions between the manufacturer and potential buyers. The Caravelle 01 prototype inherited certain advantages from the experience that was acquired with the "Grognard": drooping leading edges for improvement of high-lift effect, and the drag chute installation reducing the lengths of landing runs.

While intensive experimentation, accompanied with wind tunnel tests, has permitted high-lift devices to be waived, thus reducing the circuitry and simplifying the pilot's operating procedures, the advantages offered by the drag chute considerably increase the chances of success when it is necessary to land on an emergency strip or an ice covered runway.

On the other hand, the construction of the "Armagnac" aircraft, one of which was used as a flying test bed for high[-] thrust jet engines, has permitted Sud-Aviation to gain a considerable amount of experience with the airframe of modern airplanes.

The "fail-safe" notion—that is, the concern for the integrity of the assembly in case of failure of one or more components—has governed the philosophy of design and development throughout.

Although this term is a fairly recently [sic] addition to the technical vocabulary, it represents a very old concept, since reflections of it are found not only in current designs, but also in obsolete specifications. For instance, without anyone knowing or boasting about this consideration, the Armagnac, which returned to its base in Lyon after a bomb exploded in the aft section of its fuselage, was "fail-safe." Thus, generally speaking, we are dealing with a doctrine that has been evolved from experience and research although sometimes it is predicated on simple logic.

In fact, the application of such a principle has been marked by the absence of the minimum presence of disabling incidents. In critical areas, its application permits structural members to withstand the stresses by themselves. Attempts have also been made to have greater stresses exerted outside the jet areas.

The Danish charter airline Sterling called its Caravelle 10B3 fleet Super Caravelles. This photo was taken at Copenhagen Airport on July 12, 1969. *Courtesy of Tom Weihe*

Maximum resistance to fatigue is obtained by minimum concentration of such stresses. This led, particularly with regard to the fuselage, to research into an iso-stress design.

The critical parts of an airframe, where static and fatigue resistance are concerned, are generally located in the vicinity of structurally geometrical throws. Most of the time these are a result of installation of accommodation requirements. These discontinuities, then, must be eliminated when the main features of the structure are defined. To follow up, details encountered in designing or constructing the various structural components are managed in such a way as to improve these main features. Such precautions must often be backed by experimental research, carried out on numerous specimens of parts or assemblies. Indeed, it is established that the fatigue rupture risk greatly depends on the design of a structure and its various parts or assemblies.

Experience shows that when parts or components of a machine are subjected to small, but frequently repeated or inverted loads, breaking can occur suddenly without any strain warning about it.

Metal fatigue can be explained by the following theory. Due to inclusions and inner stresses, resulting from mechanical or heat treatment, stress peaks may exist at some points in the crystals. As the stress cycles are applied, slippage is observed in some crystals, first rapidly, then more slowly. This takes place during the first period, while, it may be said, the metal adapts itself to the fatigue. This period is not dangerous. The potential strength of the material increases through work hardening, and consequently, it can withstand greater stresses.

If the amplitude or number of cycles is too high, however, the slippage capacity is exceeded and decoherence occurs. This is the start of cracking. This second period is dangerous from the time the crack dimensions exceed those of the metal inner defects. This point being reached, the crack extends more and more rapidly, until total failure of the component occurs.

From these considerations, it can be concluded that, if the judicious choice of materials constitutes one of the main factors for success of the "fail-safe" structure policy, the fact remains that this structure must be subjected to sufficiently low and homogeneous stresses.

Sud-Aviation offered the Caravelle 11R as the only variant with a side cargo door on the main deck. It allowed the aircraft to be used in a "combi" version with both cargo and passengers. *Courtesy of www.aviationancestry.co.uk*

The low production numbers of the Caravelle 12 indicate that this final SE 210-version couldn't match the technical and operational data of its modern, next-generation competitors produced by Boeing and McDonnell Douglas. *www.aviationancestry.co.uk*

Sterling Airways was the launch customer for the largest and final version, the Caravelle 12, and used this type, which it called the "Super 12 Caravelle," on its extensive charter network. The elegant OY-SAC was photographed at Copenhagen on June 4, 1971. *Courtesy of Tom Weihe*

Sterling Airways Caravelle VIR, registered OY-SBZ, while being prepared for another charter flight from Copenhagen Airport to a Mediterranean holiday destination on August 8, 1974. *Tom Weihe*

CHAPTER 3
DO YOU SPEAK FRENCH?
THE CHALLENGES OF SELLING A REVOLUTIONARY AIRLINER

Two Finnair Caravelle 10B3s at Helsinki-Vantaa Airport in the summer of 1973.
Courtesy of Finnish Aviation Museum

When the established aircraft manufacturers Airbus and Boeing, who are very familiar to their potential customers, offer a newly developed jetliner in the twenty-first century, the biggest challenge is usually to convince the customers of its more or less obvious economic advantages. They fall back on an existing network for product support, offer power plants from renowned manufacturers who have been known in aircraft construction for decades, and have a global network with which to provide technical and operational support to their customers. The situation was quite different in the mid-1950s, when the two prototypes of the Caravelle were launched. None of the circumstances described above applied to the revolutionary jetliner. Sud-Aviation was a completely unknown manufacturer on the world stage of aviation, which in 1957, even as development of the Caravelle was going on, had emerged from the merger of SNCASE and SNCASO, which had likewise been overshadowed by the big names in aircraft construction. The jet engine was an absolute novelty, whose economic viability was doubted by numerous aviation experts, as was the

Unfortunately, it is no longer possible to look out of a teardrop-shaped S.E. 210 cabin window during flight. *Courtesy of Finnish Aviation Museum*

construction of jets in general—the reputation of which had been permanently tarnished by two disasters resulting from metal fatigue and the subsequent grounding of the de Havilland 106 Comet in 1954. The young Sud-Aviation had no sales offices, no worldwide customer service, no spare-parts warehouses on other continents, only a few contacts with airlines, and, as is still common in many French companies today, virtually no employees with foreign-language skills. So how could an excellent product be marketed globally under these conditions, in a predominantly non-Francophone world?

As so often in life, the later success of this aircraft type was due to a combination of skill, diligence, and a good portion of luck. At first, however, the Caravelle seemed destined to remain a slow seller. The situation seemed so hopeless that Sud-Aviation reckoned with a maximum production of twenty aircraft. Apart from an order placed on February 3, 1956, by the state-owned airline Air France as the first customer for twelve firm orders (plus twelve options), the pages of the order books were empty. But that was soon to change radically. In the mid-1950s, Scandinavian Airlines System (SAS) had just taken delivery of its first

Convair CV-440 Metropolitan piston-powered aircraft for European routes, and salesmen for the latest generation of turboprop aircraft were literally lining up at the SAS headquarters in Stockholm. Lockheed offered the L-188 Electra, Vickers its Vanguard and the latest version of the Viscount. But the news from Toulouse of the first flight of the Caravelle jet made the SAS engineers curious. Although Sud-Est Aviation had never before designed a passenger aircraft, apart from the unconvincing four-engine, propeller-driven S.E. 2010 Armagnac, the first group set off from Scandinavia for southern France in autumn 1955. The SAS employees wanted to see the new wonder jet with their own eyes. The team was led by Knut Hagrup, then deputy head of the technical department and later SAS president (1969–1978). For more than two weeks, the delegation members questioned the Caravelle engineers about all the technical details of the aircraft and meticulously scrutinized page after page of the construction plans. The Scandinavians were enthusiastic when they returned to Stockholm. Both in terms of design and the expected costs per seat-kilometer, the elegant jet scored surprisingly well in their assessment.

SAS management also took positive note of the discount on the purchase price offered by Sud-Est Aviation should the "Flying Vikings" sign on as the second launch customer after Air France. But the airline's board of directors and supervisory board still could not make up their minds to acquire the revolutionary S.E. 210. The new jet engine and the technologies applied for the first time to the Caravelle seemed too advanced for the numerous skeptics in the company to fall silent so quickly. A second group led by the technical director of Saab Aircraft Works, Lars Brising, flew to Toulouse—and returned to Sweden with the same, positive result as the first team. SAS pilots also had several opportunities to put the prototype through its paces in demonstration flights. They, too, were enthusiastic about the jet's flight characteristics. To be absolutely sure that the Caravelle would withstand even the harshest Scandinavian winter, Sud-Est Aviation flew the second prototype with the registration F-BHHI to Luleå in northern Sweden. After a night outdoors, in temperatures below minus 30 degrees Celsius (−22° F), the systems and engines started up the next morning without any problems. The Caravelle had also passed this endurance test with flying colors. Finally,

the SAS management wanted to get their own impression of the new miracle aircraft and took off on another test flight. The flight route led from Copenhagen to Hamburg and back to the Danish capital. Only after this short trip were the VIP guests around the then SAS president Åke Rusck finally sure: this is our future aircraft type for short- and medium-haul routes! On May 25, 1957, the SAS board of directors took the formal decision to initially purchase six S.E. 210 Caravelle Is, which was confirmed a few weeks later with an elaborately staged signing of the purchase contract in Paris. The jubilation among the employees of the former Sud-Est Aviation, which in the meantime had merged with the Société Nationale de Constructions Aéronautiques du Sud-Ouest (SNCASE) into Sud-Aviation, knew no bounds. The SAS order had considerable prestige value, since the Scandinavians were considered technological trendsetters in the aviation industry in the 1950s, following their pioneering work in developing polar air travel. The hoped-for signal effect was not long in coming, and Air Algérie, Alitalia, Finnair, Royal Air Maroc, and Varig soon followed with further orders. The ice had been broken!

SAS Caravelle III, registered SE-DAI, was christened "Alrik Viking" and equipped with 12 seats in First Class and 74 in Tourist Class at the time when this photo was taken. The Caravelle is seen here during its turn-around at Copenhagen Airport. *Courtesy of Tom Weihe*

Above and next page: Caravelle history in photos and documents. The photo captures the signing of the contract between SAS and Sud-Aviation for the initial purchase of six S.E. 210s in 1957—and next to it is the document shown in the photo, which has been preserved to this day.
Above image courtesy of SAS; two images on page 40 courtesy of Thomas Rosenqvist

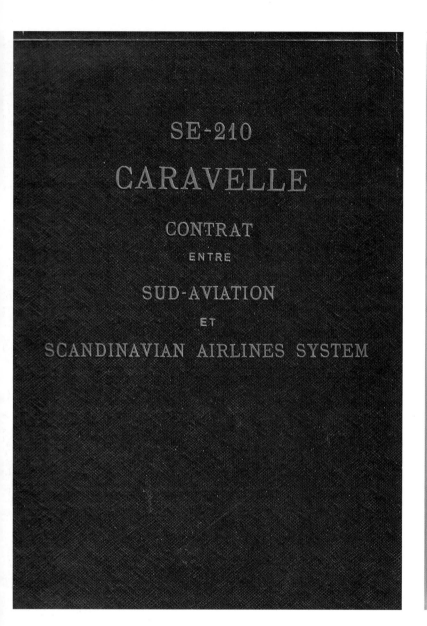

SE-210

CARAVELLE

CONTRAT

ENTRE

SUD-AVIATION

ET

SCANDINAVIAN AIRLINES SYSTEM

Between SUD-AVIATION, Société Nationale de Constructions Aéronautiques, Société Anonyme, the Head Office of which is in PARIS, 37 Boulevard de Montmorency, represented by Mr. Georges HEREIL, Président Directeur Général, who elects domicile at said Head Office (hereinafter referred to as the "Manufacturer"),

party of the first part,

and SCANDINAVIAN AIRLINES SYSTEM, the Head Office of which is in STOCKHOLM 40, represented by Mr. HENNING THRONE-HOLST, ~~President and~~ General Manager, who elects domicile at said Head Office *and Mr. Per M. Hansson, Chairman of the Board*

(hereinafter referred to as the "Buyer"),

party of the second part,

The following has been agreed:

The S.E. 210 prototype F-BHHH was painted in SAS colors in early 1959 and was made available to the airline for route trials and pilot training. *Courtesy of SAS Museum*

Sud-Aviation did not leave it at this PR success, however, and sent F-BHHI on a sales tour of South and North America as early as April 18, 1957, two years before the American FAA granted Caravelle its type certification. A total of 47,852 kilometers were flown in sixty-nine days and thirty-four legs. The aircraft took off on ninety-four flights, sixty of which were for invited guests to experience a jet flight. Destinations in South America were Recife, Rio de Janeiro, São Paulo, Porto Alegre, Buenos Aires, Belem, and Caracas. In North America, Miami, Houston, Dallas, Kansas City, St. Louis, Chicago, Denver, Salt Lake City, Los Angeles, San Francisco, Seattle, Grand Rapids, Atlanta, Washington, DC, New York, and Montreal were on the flight schedule before the aircraft returned to Paris, crossing the North Atlantic after a refueling stop in Gander. The Caravelle's reliability was demonstrated not only by the fact that not a single one of the scheduled landings on the American tour was delayed for technical reasons—but also by the fact that on June 28 of that year, just three days after returning to France, it set off on another successful sales tour to northern Europe. In addition to Caravelle orders from the South American carrier VARIG and the US airline United as a direct consequence of the aircraft's presentation at their largest hubs, the trip to the Americas also laid the foundation for later orders by Cruzeiro do Sul and Panair do Brasil, also Brazilian airlines.

On February 28, 1959, the S.E. 210 prototype 02, rented by SAS for a month, arrived in Stockholm-Bromma for intensive pilot training. Under the direction of the two training captains Gösta Carls and H. E. Fugl-Svendsen, the first Caravelle pilot corps was trained on this aircraft, which was temporarily painted in full SAS colors, to the extent that flight operations could begin as planned. The instructors undertook training flights to Copenhagen and Oslo, for example, as well as to the Swedish regional airports of Visby, Norrköping, and Malmö. On April 13, 1959, the wife of the then SAS president, Ilse Rusck, christened the first SAS aircraft, with the construction number 03, with the name Finn Viking in Toulouse at exactly twelve noon with the obligatory bottle of champagne. This aircraft took off on its maiden flight from Copenhagen to Beirut just a few days later, on April 26, 1959. SAS thus had the honor of being the world's first airline to operate a Caravelle in scheduled service, even before Air France. Perhaps this was the French company's way of thanking the SAS management, without whose foresight this revolutionary design would probably have been denied commercial success. In the 1959–60 winter timetable, the SAS Caravelle route network already included twenty-three cities in seventeen countries, which meant that in the short term, Scandinavian Airlines System served more destinations with jet aircraft than any other airline around the globe.

As briefly described in the previous chapter, Trans World Airlines (TWA) was also interested in a Caravelle order, which was described at length in the TWA staff newspaper Skyliner on September 18, 1967. It stated that the first example of the 10A version, called La Nouvelle Caravelle (the New Caravelle), with General Electric CJ805-23C "aft-fan" engines, would join the fleet from January 1963 and that the order would be completed by July of that year. The contract between Sud-Aviation and the airline, which included fifteen options in addition to the twenty firm orders, was announced by TWA president Charles C. Tillinghast Jr. back on September 7 of that year, following the conclusion of negotiations between Sud-Aviation managing director Georges Héreil and Donald Douglas Jr., president of Douglas Aircraft Co. Neil Burgess, general manager of the Commercial Engine Department of the General Electric Company, completed the celebratory quartet. TWA indicated that it would fly La Nouvelle Caravelle with either sixty-eight first-class or alternatively eighty-five tourist-class seats. As heavily advertised by Douglas and Sud-Aviation, the Caravelle 10A would have been able to operate even from short 5,000-foot runways, bringing jet service to smaller airports. By the summer of 1963, after delivery of the last aircraft ordered, the entire TWA fleet, it was planned, would have consisted of ninety-three jets of various types serving seventy destinations in the US and twenty-three international destinations.

Trained eyes will recognize it—the Caravelle prototype on the apron of Seattle-Tacoma Airport on the American West Coast. SEA-TAC Airport was one of many destinations on the Caravelle's North and South American sales tour in 1957. *Courtesy of Ministério da Defesa / Comando da Aeronáutica / Museu Aeroespacial, Rio de Janeiro*

VARIG was the first customer for the Caravelle in Latin America and initially operated its aircraft on routes to the United States, but later also on other routes within South America and on Brazilian domestic routes. *Courtesy of Ministério da Defesa / Comando da Aeronáutica / Museu Aeroespacial, Rio de Janeiro*

TWA also expected the GE CJ805-23C engines alone to improve fuel efficiency by 12 percent and increase takeoff thrust by 40 percent compared to the previous Caravelle models powered by Rolls-Royce Avon engines.

TWA not only had shown interest in La Nouvelle Caravelle but had been closely following the S.E. 210 project since its early years. Caravelle chief designer Pierre Satre received a delegation from TWA, the first ever from an American carrier. It visited Toulouse even before the prototype's maiden flight and informed itself in detail about the technical details of the prototype on the spot. The delegation was led by Robert W. Rummel, who had been Howard Hughes's personal advisor at TWA for eighteen years. In his book Howard Hughes and TWA, he describes the airline's interest in the Caravelle and the reason why the purchase of the Caravelle 10A, which had been optimized for TWA, ultimately fell through: "It was not purchased, however, due to TWA's financial reversals experienced as an aftermath of Hughes's untoward actions during the later years of his control."

Close up of the Caravelle 10R flight simulator instrument panel located at the TFC European Airline Services flight academy in the German city of Essen. The SE 210-version intended for TWA would have had a similar cockpit layout. *Author*

CARAVELLE

The finest medium range jetliner the world over

Can get into and out of any 5000 foot airport

Now, by flying Caravelles, airlines can provide pure jet service on many routes where the big jets are barred.

Not only does Caravelle have short runway requirements, but it can operate with minimum airport facilities. It carries its own built-in loading stairs and can start its twin-jet engines from its own airborne batteries.

Caravelle can fly profitably over routes from 200 to 1400 miles with as few as 28 passengers aboard. High rates of climb and descent plus jet speeds result in short block times.

It fits the Douglas tradition ...dependable, durable, and an airline profitmaker.

LANDING DISTANCE 3600 FEET

Designed and built by SUD AVIATION

Sold and serviced by DOUGLAS AIRCRAFT

Sud-Aviation had placed great hope in cooperation with the US aircraft manufacturer Douglas. The cooperative arrangement failed, not least due to the absence of Caravelle sales and the development of the Douglas DC-9, which was a direct competitor for the Caravelle. *Courtesy of www. aviationancestry.co.uk*

The Caravelle initially had a servo-hydraulic flight control system made in the British plant of the US aircraft manufacturer Lockheed. *Courtesy of www.aviationancestry.co.uk*

The 'Caravelle'

More than 100 Sud-Aviation Caravelles are on order for 9 airlines. The Caravelle, with its rear mounted engines and 'clean wing', has set the fashion for the next generation of jet-powered transports.

Right from the inception of the Caravelle, the design has incorporated the Lockheed Hydraulic system—pumps, control valves, accumulators, selector valves, duplicated powered flying controls to all surfaces and associated equipment.

Throughout, the Lockheed equipment continues to provide service equal to the brilliance of the aircraft itself.

ONE OF THE
AUTOMOTIVE
PRODUCTS

ALL-BRITISH
Lockheed
REGD. TRADE MARK

In September 1961, TWA announced the firm order for twenty Caravelle 10As and options on fifteen more in its staff magazine Skyliner. However, the order was canceled by TWA for financial reasons before the first aircraft was delivered. *Courtesy of TWA Museum*

SKYLINER

PUBLISHED BI-WEEKLY FOR TWA EMPLOYEES

You Name It!
See Back Page

VOL. 24, NO. 18   SEPTEMBER 18, 1961

CAB Inquiry Seeks Cause Of CHI Crash

CHICAGO—The Civil Aeronautics Board and other interested agencies are investigating the crash of TWA Flight 529 on September 1 nine miles west of Midway Airport with the loss of all 73 passengers and a crew of five. As yet no reason for the tragic accident has been determined.

The 049 tourist configuration Constellation left Boston at 7:45 p.m. on August 31 with stops scheduled at Idlewild, Pittsburgh, Midway, Las Vegas, Los Angeles, and San Francisco. Only minutes after the 2 a.m. takeoff from Midway, the plane crashed into a cornfield in suburban Clarendon Hills, Illinois. There were no casualties on the ground.

The Los Angeles-based TWA crew members who were lost were:

Captain James Sanders, 41, with TWA since 1945

First Officer Dale Tarrant, 31, with TWA since 1955

Flight Engineer James Newlin, 38, with TWA since 1951

Hostess Nanette Fidger, 20, with TWA since May, 1961

Hostess (Mrs.) Barbara Pearson, 25, with TWA since 1957

A team of maintenance and transportation officials, headed by Floyd D. Hall, senior vice president and system general manager; R. M. Dunn, vice president-technical services; J. E. Frankum, vice president and general transportation manager, and Robert B. Mueller, assistant vice president-flight operations, flew from Kansas City to Chicago aboard a special flight to assist federal investigators. John E. Harrington, regional general manager-transportation, served as TWA coordinator on the scene.

Soon after the tragedy, President Tillinghast issued the following message:

"My deepest personal sympathy and the sympathies of every member of the TWA organization go out to the families of passengers and crew members who lost their

(Continued on Page Three)

"LA NOUVELLE CARAVELLE," advanced version of the famed French Caravelle series, will join TWA's fleet starting in January of 1963. Twenty of the jets, to be powered by the American-made GE CJ-805-23C afftan engine, are on order, with an option for 15 more.

New GE Aftfan Engines Power TWA Caravelles

NEW YORK—The General Electric CJ-805-23C engine for TWA's La Nouvelle Caravelle has been uprated to deliver more thrust at climb power settings and consume less fuel during cruise.

Increases of up to 8.2 percent in climb thrust will enable the high performance Caravelle, built by Sud Aviation, to reach an altitude of 30,000 feet in 18 minutes at full gross weight. Reduction in time to climb means faster block times and lower operating costs.

Thrust at maximum cruise has been increased as much as 7 percent with an attendant increase in fuel consumption of no more than 1.3 percent. At some operating altitudes, fuel consumption is actually improved even though thrust is increased. When combined with other aircraft improvements, this additional cruise thrust results in an increase of more than 5 percent in maximum speed capability of TWA's Caravelle 10-A.

These engine performance improvements have been accomplished by design modifications to the major engine components. The modifications have been tested extensively at the GE plant near Cincinnati, and official FAA certification testing has already been completed.

Intensive flight test experience has demonstrated the reliability and performance of the CJ-805-23C. In February, 1960, a leased U.S. Air Force RB-66 powered by the GE aft turbofans, made the first fan-powered flight in this country.

The company also purchased a Caravelle from Sud Aviation for further flight testing of the engines and demonstration of their compatibility with the airframe. In accumulating 400 engine flight hours, the GE Caravelle has established an excellent reliability record. During a recent European demonstration tour, there were no delays or cancellations in 64 scheduled departures from 16 different airports in 11 different countries.

The TWA Medical Units have discontinued inoculation service for employees and their family members taking personal trips overseas. The demand for immunization has increased to the point where the service can no longer be provided by the company. Yellow fever shots will continue to be given by the medical unit when required.

Twenty Caravelle Jets Ordered From Sud Co.; 1963 Delivery Planned

NEW YORK—Twenty jet aircraft of a type to be known as "La Nouvelle Caravelle," newest, fastest and most advanced of the famed Caravelle series, have been ordered by TWA from Sud Aviation Company of Toulouse, France, it was announced September 7 by President Charles C. Tillinghast, Jr. The order includes an option for 15 additional aircraft of the same type.

"La Nouvelle (new) Caravelle," powered by the American-made General Electric CJ-805-23C afftan jet engines, will join the TWA fleet beginning in January of 1963. Delivery of the 20 planes is scheduled to be completed by July.

President Tillinghast's announcement was made at the conclusion of negotiations with Georges Hereil, president and director general of Sud; Donald Douglas, Jr., president of Douglas Aircraft Co., U. S. sales-service representative for Sud, and Neil Burgess, general manager of General Electric Company, commercial engine department.

TWA will pay nearly $100,000,000 for the Caravelles including spare engines and parts. They will be equipped with electronic navigational aids including distance measuring equipment (DME) and radar. Financing arrangements are being completed, President Tillinghast said.

TWA now flies 27 Boeing 707s, both domestic and international models, and is completing delivery on its fleet of 20 Convair 880s. Twenty-six Boeing 707 turbofan jets are on order for delivery next year. In addition, TWA is currently leasing four Boeing 720B models, pending delivery of the turbofan 707 fleet.

The TWA Caravelles (Model 10A) represent substantial changes in the original Caravelles which have been in scheduled operation for more than two years. These changes consist of many aerodynamic improvements which give the Caravelle 10A greater speed and range.

Passenger capacity ranges from 68 first class to 85 tourist.

"La Nouvelle Caravelle" is designed to operate from 5,000-foot runways and will permit TWA to offer jet service to more cities. Its operating range is up to about 1,000 miles with a top cruising speed of nearly 550 miles an hour. Caravelle's normal operating altitude will be about 30,000 feet.

The TWA jet will be the first Caravelle equipped with General Electric afftan engines. The engines will be mounted on the rear of the fuselage with a resulting low sound level in the cabin and considerably less noise that might disturb residents of communities adjacent to jet airports.

A self-contained passenger loading ramp which retracts into the tail of the plane and wide-view cabin windows are among the Caravelle features.

Delivery of the Caravelles will give TWA a diversified fleet of 93 jets to serve its 50,000 miles of routes through 70 U. S. cities and 23 world centers abroad.

Here is a reminder that September 25 is the renewal date for aviation insurance policies available to TWA employees through the Continental Casualty Company.

All such policies written through TWA carry the same renewal date. Employees interested may obtain applications from the Insurance Division, Treasury Department, 1735 Baltimore, Kansas City.

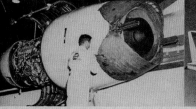

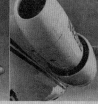

TWA'S NOUVELLE CARAVELLE will be powered by the American-made General Electric CJ-805-23C afftan engine. GE estimates that the aft turbofan adds 40 percent more takeoff power and improves fuel economy by more than 12 percent. These pictures of GE's own Caravelle, which has tested the new engine since last December, point up the "clamshell" type thrust reverser. In landing, the clamshell doors swing shut to reverse the direction of the engine exhaust for shortening the landing roll. The closed doors force 38 percent of the engine's thrust in the opposite direction, which results in a braking action. In flight the clamshell doors fair neatly into the nacelles, eliminating any thrust loss.

A FAVORITE WITH CHARTER AIRLINES

Caravelles flew on five continents—North and South America, Europe, Africa, and Asia. Factory-new machines were first delivered to the large, often-state-owned carriers of a respective country, before secondary airlines also placed orders with Sud-Aviation and acquired used machines at favorable terms from the "flag carriers." Two prominent exceptions were the Netherlands and the Federal Republic of Germany. Neither the Dutch national airline KLM nor Deutsche Lufthansa AG ordered brand-new S.E. 210s, although they were intensively courted by Sud-Aviation as potential customers. Both airlines did, however, temporarily rent Caravelles from other airlines to bridge capacity bottlenecks. In the case of KLM, these were Finnair aircraft, while Lufthansa also made use of S.E. 210s from Finnair and Air France. Nevertheless, fourteen aircraft of the type were registered in the Netherlands and ten in the German aviation registry—and thus more than in Algeria, Morocco, or Portugal. The solution to the riddle has two names: Transavia and LTU. The first was Lufttransport Unternehmen GmbH (LTU), which was entered in the German commercial register on October 20, 1955. The Düsseldorf-based holiday airline entered the jet age on February 12, 1965, when it officially took delivery of the Caravelle III acquired from Sud-Aviation with the registration number D-ABAF and name Nordrhein-Westfalen. Previously, the aircraft with construction number 21 had been used by Finnair with the registration OH-LEA and the name Sinilintu. The next Caravelle in the LTU fleet was the factory-new Series III D-ABAM, leased from the manufacturer on December 6, 1966, before the airline relied on a mix of five factory-new and used Caravelle 10Rs with the registrations D-ABAF, D-ABAP, D-ABAV, D-ABAW, and D-ANYL. Based at Düsseldorf Airport as a "home carrier" since 1961, LTU developed over the decades into one of the most renowned German holiday airlines, in part thanks to its reliable Caravelle jets. Its history as an independent company ended only in March 2007, when Air Berlin took over 100 percent of LTU for 140 million euros. Three aircraft of the LTU Caravelle 10R fleet found a new owner in Special Air Transport (SAT), also of Germany. After SAT was transferred to Germania Fluggesellschaft in 1986, Caravelle D-ABAW remained in its fleet until November of that year. Aero Lloyd, based at Frankfurt Airport, acquired three Caravelle 10Rs—D-AAST, D-ABAK, and D-ACVK—on the used-aircraft market. The Dutch airline Transavia put seven secondhand Caravelle IIIs and as many VI-Rs into service from 1969 onward, stationing them at Amsterdam-Schiphol Airport.

In October 1973, the Organization of Arab Petroleum Exporting Countries, or OAPEC, imposed a partial oil embargo on those countries that supported Israel in the Yom Kippur War—including the United States. When the embargo was lifted in March 1974, the global price of oil was an incredible 400 percent higher. The airlines were so badly affected by the rising cost of jet fuel in parallel with the price of crude oil that it meant the end of service for some types of aircraft on the main air traffic routes—such as the gas-guzzling, four-engine Convair 880. Even for the Caravelle III, which consumed 930 US gallons per hour, there was only one chance for its continued use: the number of passenger seats had to be drastically increased. Expressed in figures—a Caravelle III consumed more than 1.05 US gallons (4 liters) of jet fuel per passenger in a two-class version over a distance of 54 nautical miles, while for a more modern Douglas DC-9 jet of the 1970s, the figure was around 0.92 US gallons (3.5 liters). Currently, the consumption of a comparable high-tech regional jet from Airbus or Embraer is less than 0.66 US gallons (2.5 liters) per passenger over the identical distance. As a reaction to the "oil price shock" at the time, the Caravelle IIIs of the Scandinavian airline SAS, for example, were converted from twelve first-class and seventy-four tourist-class seats to a pure economy version with ninety-four seats. Many other airlines followed this example. Only in this way was it possible to at least partially compensate for the higher fuel costs by selling more tickets. But even this attempt to operate the Caravelle III to VI economically with Rolls-Royce Avon engines had its limits, and so most of the large

The red-and-white livery of the German charter airline LTU looked particularly elegant on its S.E. 210 10Rs. *Author's collection*

The German holiday carrier LTU started with the Caravelle III into the jet age. Pictured on this airline issued postcard motive is an aircraft showing the false registration D-ABAP. The two LTU SE 210 III were in reality registered D-ABAF and D-ABAM. The registration D-ABAP was used for a later Caravelle 10R, construction number 235. *LTU / author's collection*

network airlines around the globe parted with their first-generation S.E. 210s at the beginning of the 1970s, replacing them with more-economical Boeing and Douglas jets such as the 737 and DC-9. Some of the aircraft were scrapped, and others were sold cheaply to charter airlines with a lower cost structure—or their own charter departments equipped with decommissioned Caravelle jets. For example, thirteen jets from the United Airlines fleet went to the Danish charter airline Sterling, based in the Danish capital of Copenhagen. Air France and the Belgian airline Sabena handed over some of their fleets to their own holiday airlines Air Charter International and Sobelair, respectively, while Swissair aircraft found new employment with charter airlines in the Netherlands, France, and Switzerland.

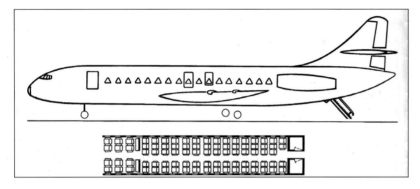

For a tourist-oriented holiday airline such as LTU, the offer of a first-class service on its Caravelles was decidedly unusual. As can be seen in this contemporary seating plan, the first three rows, with a total of twelve seats, were reserved for first class. The service offered was so outstanding that even heads of state flew on LTU Caravelle jets. *Author's collection*

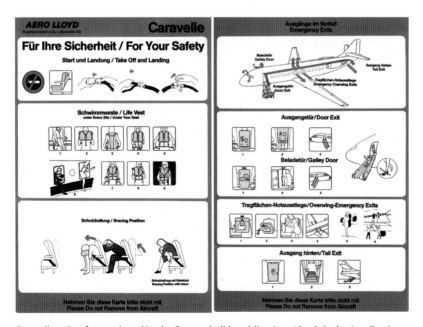

Caravelle 10R safety card used by the German holiday airline Aero Lloyd. *Author's collection*

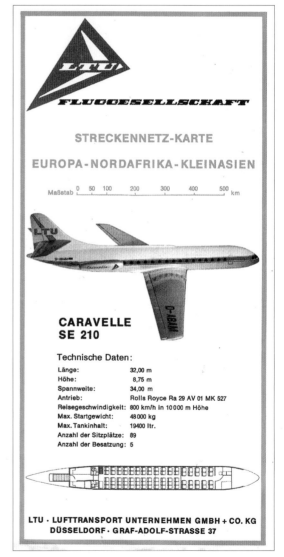

The cover of a LTU route map shows their Caravelle in a first and economy class cabin layout. *Author's collection*

In addition to LTU, the German charter airlines SAT and Aero Lloyd also included the Caravelle 10R in their fleets. *Courtesy of Christian Käufer, author's collection, and Dr. John Provan*

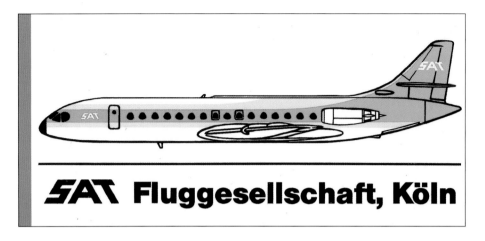

Air France transferred this and seven other Caravelle IIIs to its wholly owned holiday subsidiary airline Air Charter International (ACI) in 1970–71. The last aircraft was not retired until 1983. They included this S.E. 210, originally delivered to Air France on May 4, 1962, as F-BJTG. *Courtesy of Tom Weihe*

The Caravelle III shown here with the French registration F-BRUJ is another example of aircraft of this type that were taken out of service by the major carriers in the 1970s—and subsequently entered service with charter airlines. It was originally leased factory-new as LN-KLN by SAS in 1965 and found its second operator in Trans-Union from March 15, 1970. *Courtesy of Tom Weihe*

Compagnie de Transport Aerienne (CTA) was a Swiss charter airline based in Geneva that was founded on September 28, 1978, and initially carried passengers with four "Super Caravelle" S.E. 210 10Rs. As a special feature, CTA operated its Caravelles not only with the usual charter seating, but also in an executive version. *Author's collection*

Sterling Airways of Denmark acquired this S.E. 210 VI-R, previously operated by United as N1010U Ville de Strasbourg, on January 7, 1972. It was one of thirteen that Sterling secured from United after its retirement. *Courtesy of Tom Weihe*

The perfect combination: the classic lines of a great jetliner and a classic livery. Demonstrated on this SE 210 III of Air France during a visit of Copenhagen Airport on August 20, 1968. *Tom Weihe*

CHAPTER 4
PIONEERS OF THE JET AGE

The following list includes Air France, SAS, VARIG, Finnair, Air Algérie, Royal Air Maroc, Swissair, and Alitalia, the first eight airline customers of the S.E. 210, as well as other operators from the early days that were of significance in their region. Of the 282 S.E. 210s built, sixty-four were lost in accidents—and many involved the loss of life. The Caravelle dates from an analog era before the advent of computers, and so the crews of the time could only dream of today's glass cockpits and their safety features. Most of these accidents were due to the fact that onboard and ground systems that are taken for granted today, such as air traffic control with seamless radar coverage and weather forecasting, ground-proximity warning systems, traffic collision avoidance systems (TCAS), and GPS for exact geographical orientation, had not yet been developed.

Nevertheless, the Caravelle was a comparatively safe commercial aircraft by the standards of the time. For example, between 1946 and 1973, the British airline BEA recorded forty-four total losses without having a Caravelle in service, in which 538 people lost their lives! The risk of losing one's life in an air accident was thus much higher

Above and opposite: Iberia of Spain, Finnair of Finland, Sabena of Belgium, and JAT of the former Yugoslavia were significant European airlines that maintained substantial fleets of Caravelle of various versions. *Courtesy of Tom Weihe*

than in the present. In 2017, the US National Center for Health Statistics found that the probability of dying in a plane crash that year was 1 in 188,394—while the probability of dying in a car crash was 1 in 103. The year 2017 was also the first in aviation history that not a single person died in a passenger jet flight!

AFRICA

AIR ALGÉRIE

When the Société Algérienne de Construction Aéronautique, Air Algérie for short, was founded in 1947, today's Algeria was still a colony of France. In the midst of the war of independence, the first S.E. 210 Caravelle I, with the French registration F-OBNH, was delivered to Air Algérie on January 14, 1960. After its conversion to Series III standard in May 1961, it was sold to the Brazilian airline VARIG on December 15, 1961, where it received the registration PP-VJI. After gaining independence from France and the establishment of the Democratic Republic of Algeria, the remaining three Caravelle IIIs and two Caravelle VI-Ns were registered in the Algerian aviation registry. The aircraft were used mainly on routes between the former colonial power France and Algeria. The tragedy involving the Air Algérie Caravelle VI-N 7T-VAK on July 26, 1969, revealed a general design shortcoming of this type, and not only of the VI-N. Its highly flammable oxygen tanks were placed next to the failure-prone onboard batteries, which often overheated and caught fire. Together with the cabin interior, made of wood and plastic, this was a disastrous breeding ground for a fire to flare up in the cabin, which was responsible for the fire on board 7T-VAK. The fire and the toxic gases it produced led to the crash of the aircraft and the death of most of those on board—only the pilots were able to save themselves.

Air Algérie was one of the first Caravelle customers, along with Air France, SAS, VARIG, Finnair, Royal Air Maroc, Swissair, and Alitalia. *Courtesy of www. aviationancenstry.co.uk*

ROYAL AIR MAROC

The Kingdom of Morocco, located in northwestern Africa, gained independence from the colonial powers of France and Spain in 1956. Royal Air Maroc, or RAM for short, officially began operations the following year as the kingdom's national airline. It entered the jet age on May 11, 1960, with a Caravelle 1A, which was later converted to Caravelle III standard, and three other aircraft delivered from the factory as Caravelle IIIs. Following the S.E. 210, RAM procured Boeing 707s for long-haul flights and Boeing 737s and 727s as short- and medium-haul jets and successors to the Caravelle. Royal Air Maroc lost two Caravelle aircraft in 1970 and 1973. Two aircraft, one of its own Caravelle IIIs with the registration CN-CCV and one VI-N (OO-SRD) leased from the Belgian airline Sobelair, were lost in controlled flight into terrain crashes due to a loss of orientation in fog and darkness.

Aircraft CN-CCZ, shown here, was a Caravelle III operated by Royal Air Maroc between June 1965 and November 1976. For a long time it was used as a training aircraft at Casablanca airport—but has since been scrapped. *Courtesy of W. Soltermann collection, bsl-mlh-planes.net*

EUROPE

AERO OY / FINNAIR

Founded as Aero OY on November 1, 1923—and operating as Finnair since 1960—Finnair is one of the world's oldest airlines. With its initial Caravelle order in 1957, Aero OY became one of the first customers for the elegant jetliner, which in 1960 became its first jet type ever. The airline operated a total of fifteen Caravelle IAs, which were later converted to Series III standard, Caravelle VI-Rs, and more-advanced Caravelle 10B3s with Pratt & Whitney engines. Finnair was the launch customer for the latter version—which Finnair called the "Super Caravelle." The last aircraft did not leave the fleet until 1984 and were replaced by McDonnell Douglas MD-80s, temporarily making the airline, with its DC-8s, DC-9s, DC-10s, MD-80s, and MD-11s, an exclusive McDonnell Douglas customer. Currently, Finnair's fleet consists primarily of Airbus A320 family aircraft and A350s for long-haul routes. In addition, Brazilian Embraer E190s are operated by regional partner NORRA (Nordic Regional Airlines) on behalf of Finnair. Finnair is a member of the Global One World Alliance and thus a partner of American Airlines and British Airways.

Arrival of the first Finnair Caravelle 1A with the registration OH-LEA at Helsinki Airport on February 22, 1960. The aircraft with the construction number 21 was converted to Series III standard in 1961 and sold to the German charter airline LTU in August 1964, becoming its first jet. *Courtesy of Finnish Aviation Museum*

AIR FRANCE AND AIR INTER

The first commercial flight by an SAS Caravelle was followed by the aircraft's debut in Air France service on May 6, 1959, on the Paris-Orly–Istanbul route. The jet age had now finally arrived in France on medium-haul routes. With up to forty-six aircraft, the French state carrier not only operated the largest fleet of Caravelle aircraft but also used them for the longest period of time of all its early customers. The last S.E. 210 III did not leave the Air France fleet until 1981, after more than two decades in scheduled service.

Air Inter, the French domestic airline in which Air France played a major role, was founded in 1954 to provide a rapid link between the French departements and Paris, the country's political and economic center. The airline ceased to exist when it was merged with Air France in April 1997. Its hub was located at Orly airport in the French capital, from where there was a dense network of connections. In addition to eighteen Caravelle IIIs, Air Inter also operated the largest and last version of this type on its network with its thirteen Caravelle 12s, called "Super Douze." It also temporarily leased three Caravelle VI-Ns and one VI-R. The first Series III aircraft joined Air Inter in 1967 and remained part of the fleet until April 1983. After the S.E. 210 became the first passenger jet to be certified for Category III approaches (horizontal visibility: 150

The Air France S.E. 210 shown here, with the registration F-BOHA and aircraft name Comte de Nice, was photographed at Stockholm-Arlanda airport in August 1978. *Courtesy of AirNikon Collection, Pima Air and Space Museum*

meters / decision height: 15 meters) on December 28, 1968, on January 9, 1969, an Air Inter aircraft made the first CAT III landing by a scheduled passenger flight. The Caravelle 12 with the registration F-GCVK closed out the S.E. 210's service with a final scheduled flight in August 1991. The aircraft that remained in the fleet until the end were officially retired in September of that year and replaced by Airbus A320s. In the twenty-four years of service, not a single passenger on board an Air Inter Caravelle was injured. The same was true of the Dassault Mercure jets, operated exclusively by Air Inter, which also did not have a single accident resulting in personal injury during the course of their use in scheduled service.

Rolf Keller took this photo of an Air Inter Caravelle 12 on May 21, 1987, at the Basle-Mulhouse-Freiburg (BSL) trinational Euro Airport. Aircraft F-GCVK has been preserved to this day and is used for training purposes at the Institut Aéronautique Amaury de la Grange in Merville Calonne, France. *Courtesy of Rolf Keller, bsl-mlh-planes.net*

ALITALIA

After the first national Italian airline, Ala Littoria S.A., founded in August 1934, went under in the turmoil of the Second World War, the Italian state, together with private investors and British European Airways (BEA), founded Aerolinee Italiane Internazionali (Alitalia) on September 16, 1946. In 1957, Linee Aeree Italiane (LAI), also founded in 1946 with the support of the US airline Trans World Airlines (TWA), was merged into Alitalia, before the jet age began in 1960 with fifteen Douglas DC-8-43s and twenty-one Caravelles of the III and VI-N versions for the newly formed Italian national airline. The first three aircraft delivered by Sud-Aviation as S.E. 210 Caravelle IIIs in 1960 were converted to VI-N version standard two years later. The airline, which now operated as Alitalia–Linee Aeree Italiane, founded Società Aerea Mediterranea (SAM) in 1959 as a subsidiary for charter flights, to which Alitalia transferred some of its own S.E. 210 Caravelle VI-N aircraft. This aircraft type was flown in the colors of Alitalia and ATI, its domestic subsidiary, as well as SAM until 1977.

Above and next page: Alitalia and its charter division SAM were frequent visitors to Copenhagen. The photograph of S.E. 210 Caravelle III I-DAXI was taken on August 20, 1968, while I-DABT of Societa Aerea Mediterranea (SAM) was captured on film at the Danish capital's airport on April 1, 1972. *Courtesy of Tom Weihe*

Alitalia used posters such as this one to attract customers for its Caravelle fleet. *Courtesy of Alitalia*

AUSTRIAN AIRLINES

After the end of the Second World War, Austria, like Germany, was initially not permitted by the victorious Allied powers to operate its own airline. It was not until Austria regained air sovereignty, after the Soviet Union had also agreed to this on April 15, 1955, that the way was cleared for the Alpine republic to create a national airline. In the same year, negotiations began with the Dutch airline KLM and the Scandinavian SAS for the joint establishment of an Austrian national carrier. After turbulent discussions at the national political and economic level, Österreichische Luftverkehrs A.G.—Austrian Airlines (AUA)—was finally officially founded on September 30, 1957. The Austrian airline joined forces with SAS and the Norwegian A/S Fred. Olsen Flyselskap as airline shareholders, and it began flight operations between Vienna and London on March 31, 1958. Its fleet initially consisted of Vickers Viscount 700s from its Norwegian partner. After the acquisition of further Viscount turboprops of the larger 837 version, in 1961, a decision in principle was made to purchase pure jets of the Caravelle type. On October 29, 1962, the AUA management signed a contract with Sud-Aviation for the initial purchase of two Caravelle VI-Rs, the first of which arrived on April 20, 1963, to the cheers of the Viennese population, who had flocked en masse to Schwechat Airport. The Austrian press was full of superlatives. Among other things, the papers wrote: "It is the best medium-haul aircraft ever. And it is certainly the most beautiful, with its slender fuselage and long wings, and its two engines nestled close against the fuselage." AUA ordered a total of five aircraft, the last of which was delivered on May 19, 1965.

Austrian Airlines chose the Caravelle VI-R with thrust reversers as its entry into the jet age. On a sunny and cloudless day, OE-LCU, with its red-and-white livery, stands out perfectly against the bright-blue sky of the Danish capital, Copenhagen. *Courtesy of Tom Weihe*

SCANDINAVIAN AIRLINES SYSTEM (SAS)

SAS was founded on August 1, 1946, as a result of a merger of the four largest airlines in Scandinavia: Norwegian airline DNL, the Danish DDL, and the two Swedish airlines ABA and SILA. In keeping with the motto "Only together are we strong," the realization that none of the four partner airlines could survive alone in global competition in the long term had triumphed over national egoism. From 1957 onward, SAS gradually ordered up to twenty-one examples of the S.E. 210 in versions I, IA, and III. The first ten aircraft delivered were Series I/IA aircraft, which were upgraded in 1960–61 to Series III standard, with more-powerful Rolls-Royce R.A. 29 Mk. 527B engines. The appearance of the elegant jet triggered a veritable "Caravelle fever" in Scandinavia. The pop-up pub "Caravelle Inn" opened at Copenhagen-Kastrup Airport especially for the passengers of the Caravelle demonstration flights. The song "Caravelle Samba," composed on behalf of SAS, celebrated the elegant jet itself in a musical way. Wherever SAS opened a route with the elegant jets, the local daily newspapers were full of euphoric reports. On numerous press trips, journalists had the opportunity to get a personal impression of a flight on the new short-and-medium-haul jet. Most reports exuberantly celebrated the elegance of the aircraft, the comfort of its cabin, and the speed bestowed by the new jet engines—just as the SAS PR department had hoped. On April 13, 1959, the first S.E. 210 Caravelle I destined for SAS, with construction number 03, arrived at Stockholm-Bromma. The aircraft, christened Finn Viking, took off on its maiden flight from Copenhagen to Beirut just a few days later, on April 26, 1959. SAS thus had the honor of being the world's first airline to operate a Caravelle in scheduled service, even before Air France. Perhaps this was the French company's way of thanking the SAS management, without whose foresight this revolutionary design would probably have been denied commercial success. By the end of the 1959 summer timetable, the SAS Caravelle route network already covered twenty-two cities in seventeen countries, meaning that in the short term, Scandinavian Airlines System served more destinations with jet aircraft than any other airline around the globe.

Alongside all the euphoria, there were also tragic moments, such as the loss of the SAS Caravelle I with the registration OY-KRB on January 19, 1960—the first-ever crash involving an aircraft of this type. Flight SK871 was approaching the airport of the Turkish capital of Ankara when it crashed into a ridge and was completely destroyed. All forty-two people on board were killed. The cause was a descent below the minimum safe altitude during this critical phase of the flight, but the reason could never be fully determined. At the time, there was no ground-proximity warning system (GPWS), which is now a standard feature of commercial aircraft and warns of an unintended, and thus dangerous, descent into terrain. It was only the accumulation of information about such controlled flights into terrain (CFIT) in the 1960s, in which a fully intact aircraft was flown into an obstacle on the ground, that led to the installation requirement by the US Federal Aviation Administration (FAA) in 1974. Similarly the flight data recorder (FDR), for recording countless technical parameters during a flight, and the cockpit voice recorder (CVR), for recording conversations in the cockpit, did not yet exist on board commercial aircraft at that time. If today's FDR and CVR had been installed on board OY-KRB, the cause of the accident could certainly have been determined beyond doubt.

The Caravelle I with the registration LN-KLH, construction number 3, and aircraft name *Finn Viking* was the first S.E. 210 delivered to SAS on April 10, 1959. It was converted to Caravelle III standard in October 1960 and has been on display at the Norwegian Museum of Science and Technology in the Norwegian capital, Oslo, for many years. *Courtesy of SAS Museum*

SWISSAIR

Swissair (Schweizerische Luftverkehr AG), which was formed on March 26, 1931, from the merger of the Zurich airline Ad Astra-Aero and the Basel-based Balair, has distinguished itself throughout its existence through its technical expertise and a service of worldwide renown. Its standards also included always using the most-modern aircraft—such as the Caravelle. In 1958, SAS and Swissair entered into a close cooperation. This included commercial aspects such as joint pool flights, the technical maintenance of the fleet, and operational details. In the summer of 1961, SAS and Swissair operated twenty-six weekly connections in a joint Middle East flight schedule. These extended as far as Cairo and Bahrain, Kuwait, and Tehran. Of these, fifteen routes were operated by Swissair and eleven by SAS, of which the Scandinavians alone flew nine with their Caravelles.

In order to obtain better purchasing conditions for new aircraft as relatively small airlines, from 1958 onward SAS and Swissair jointly procured their new fleet additions in larger numbers. In the case of the S.E. 210, in concrete terms this meant that SAS acquired four aircraft from the manufacturer and initially leased them to Swissair before they were purchased by the Swiss from their northern European partner. Conversely, Swissair ordered four-engine Convair CV 990A Coronado airliners and leased two of them to SAS. The aircraft were identical in all technical details, including the decor of the interior. SAS also took over responsibility for maintaining the Swissair Caravelles. The aircraft components were overhauled in the workshops at Stockholm-Arlanda Airport, and the Rolls-Royce Avon engines in the Linta workshops near Bromma Airport, also in Stockholm. In the following years, their cooperation was expanded to include the Douglas DC-8, Douglas DC-9, and Boeing 747 models; the Airbus A300B wide-body jets; and the McDonnell Douglas DC-10. Partner airlines KLM and UTA subsequently joined to form the KSSU consortium.

The Swissair Caravelle III HB-ICY on one of its regular visits to Copenhagen, in perfect photographic weather. Saved for posterity on June 16, 1969. *Courtesy of Tom Weihe*

The use of the Caravelle by Swissair will forever be associated with one of the most tragic human disasters involving this type. With the crash of flight SR 306, the Swiss village of Hümlikon lost a fifth of its inhabitants in one fell swoop, and numerous children were orphaned. The cause of the accident was a chain of events linked to a procedure practiced over a long period of time by Swissair but not approved by Sud-Aviation or the Swiss aviation authority. On that tragic September 4, 1963, dense ground fog covered the Zurich-Kloten Airport. Visibility on the active runway was 524 feet (160 meters), 787 feet (240 meters) below the minimum required for the Caravelle. As on many previous foggy days, the aircraft with the registration HB-ICV taxied with engines at full thrust and brakes applied along the entire length of the runway to blow away the fog. The resulting tunnel then gave the crew the necessary view of the runway lights ahead of them for a few minutes. What the pilots could not have known was that the magnesium alloy used in the wheels had become so hot during this maneuver that the brake discs overheated and disintegrated while the aircraft was still on the ground. When the landing gear was retracted after takeoff, the sharp-edged remnants pierced the nearby hydraulic lines of the flight control system, and the highly flammable hydraulic fluid immediately ignited on the glowing material. Burning, and quickly out of control, the Caravelle hurtled earthward and smashed into the ground, creating a deep crater on the outskirts of Dürrenäsch. Forty three of the seventy-four people who died on the aircraft were from the Swiss village of Hümlikon, which had a total population of 217. In the village, thirty-nine children lost both parents, and five others one parent in the crash.

Thick fog like that seen in this photo prevailed on the early morning of September 4, 1963, when flight SR 306 taxied for takeoff at Zurich. The details of the disaster that unfolded moments later are part of the Swissair chapter. *Courtesy of ETH-Bibliothek Zurich, Bildarchiv / Stiftung Luftbild Schweiz / photographer: Swissair / LBS_SR03-20485 / CC BY-SA 4.0*

THE MIDDLE EAST

ALIA ROYAL JORDANIAN AIRLINES

The formation of Royal Jordanian Airlines, the national airline of the Hashemite Kingdom of Jordan, can be traced back to a decree issued by Jordan's King Hussein (1935–1999) on December 15, 1963. It is recorded that King Hussein commented: "I want our national carrier to be our ambassador of good will around the world, and a bridge across which we can exchange culture, civilization, trade, technology, friendship, and better understanding with the rest of the world." Since its privatization in December 2007, Royal Jordanian's shares have been traded on the stock exchange in Jordan's capital city of Amman. Amman-Marka Airport was the starting point of Royal Jordanian's extensive network when it operated three Caravelle 10Rs. Royal Jordanian was the launch customer for this S.E. 210 version equipped with Pratt & Whitney JT8D-1 and -7 engines. The first aircraft of the trio was delivered by Sud-Aviation to Alia on July 28, 1965, having been christened Amman. It is known that King Hussein, who was an aviation enthusiast and held a commercial pilot's license, often sat at the controls of one of the three Caravelle 10Rs himself.

This photo of a Royal Jordanian Caravelle 10R was taken at Jordan's Aqaba Airport in 1966. The aircraft were often flown by the Jordanian king himself, who held the requisite license. *Courtesy of Royal Jordanian Airlines*

MEA: MIDDLE EAST AIRLINES

Today's Middle East Airlines traces its roots back to three airlines that merged in 1963 to form Lebanon's current airline: Air Liban, MEA, and Lebanese International Airways. MEA had entered the jet age with de Havilland Comet 4s before taking delivery of three brand-new Caravelle VI-Ns (OD-AEE, OD-AEF, and OD-AEO) in 1963, but the first two were destroyed on December 28, 1968, when Israeli commandos attacked Beirut airport. Previously, Air Liban had leased one Caravelle III each from Air Algérie and Air France, and MEA had leased one Caravelle III from Air France. The latter, with the registration number OD-AEM, crashed into the sea on April 17, 1964, while on approach to Dhahran, killing all forty-two passengers and seven crew members.

Beirut-based Middle East Airlines (MEA) took delivery of three brand-new Caravelle VI-Ns from Sud-Aviation in 1963 and 1964. Among them was OD-AEE, construction number 153, which was destroyed in an Israeli commando attack on Beirut Airport on December 28, 1968. *Courtesy of Tom Weihe*

ASIA

INDIAN AIRLINES

June 15, 1953, is the joint founding date of Air India, originally launched for international air traffic, and the now-defunct Indian Airlines, established to handle domestic traffic. Indian Airlines began operations on August 1 of that year. It initially maintained a mixed fleet of propeller-driven aircraft until it became the first Indian airline to put S.E. 210 Caravelle VI-Ns into service, beginning January 1, 1964. Some of the nine aircraft purchased from the manufacturer were originally supposed to be delivered to Trans World Airlines (TWA) in the US as Caravelle 10As. After this order was canceled, they were converted to VI-N standard and delivered to Indian Airlines. In addition, three secondhand machines were purchased, giving Indian Airlines a total of twelve Caravelles. However, five of these aircraft had to be written off as total losses following accidents. These included the catastrophic accident involving VT-DWN on October 12, 1976, in which all ninety-five occupants lost their lives shortly after the aircraft took off from Bombay. The cause was a ruptured compressor blade in one of the two Rolls-Royce Avon engines, debris from which punctured the hydraulic lines of the flight controls, rendering the aircraft uncontrollable and causing it to crash. In its fifty-eight years of existence, Indian Airlines has lost a total of sixty aircraft, and 882 people their lives. Later Indian Airlines jetliners from Toulouse were the Airbus models A300B4, A319/320/321, and A330.

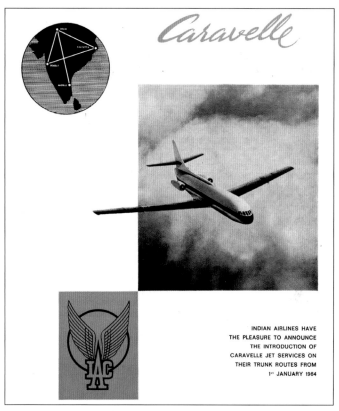

This advertisement promoted the launch of Indian Airlines' Caravelle jet routes on January 1, 1964. A total of twelve S.E. 210 VI-Ns flew in the colors of the now-defunct Indian domestic airline. *Courtesy of www.aviationancestry.co.uk*

Thai Airways International started operations in 1960 as a joint-venture between Scandinavian Airlines (30 percent) and Thai Airways (70 percent). SAS supplied Caravelle jets from its European network for its Asian start-up, including cockpit crews, and painted the aircraft in a SAS inspired livery with a touch of Thai tradition. *Thai Airways International*

THAI AIRWAYS INTERNATIONAL

Thai Airways International was officially registered on March 29, 1960, as a joint venture between the Thai airline Thai Airways Company and the Scandinavian airline SAS. The latter supported its partner in the joint operation by sending its own administrative, technical, and flight personnel from Scandinavia to Thailand. In Asia, SAS and Thai also maintained joint sales offices to save costs. As well, in the early years the fleet consisted exclusively of aircraft that were loaned to Thai Airways by SAS. These included Douglas DC-6 propeller planes and, from 1962, a Convair CV-990A Coronado, its first jet type—followed a year later by the S.E. 210. The outward sign of this cooperation was that the Thai

International jets were painted very similarly to those of SAS. The aircraft not only were leased to Thai Airways by the Scandinavians but were also partly flown by SAS pilots stationed in Bangkok. The SAS technical station at Tokyo-Haneda Airport, on the other hand, carried out mandatory periodic checks on the airline's S.E. 210s.

Just six Caravelle IIIs—HS-TGF, -TGG, -TGH, -TGI, -TGL, and -TGK—carried a Thai registration for the duration of their service with Thai International. Aircraft with the Danish and Swedish registrations OY-KRC, -KRF, SE-DAA, -DAB, and -DAC were other SAS aircraft that were temporarily operated by Thai Airways with their Scandinavian registrations. Thai Airways lost a Caravelle III when HS-TGI crashed while on approach to land at Hong Kong.

More of a publicity stunt than a regularly used "ground vehicle," this elephant is pulling a Thai Airways International S.E. 210 Caravelle III across the airport apron. *Courtesy of Thai Airways International*

The first Thai Airways International jetliners were three S.E. 210 transferred from SAS to the subsidiaries operational hub at Bangkok airport. *Thai Airways International*

THE AMERICAS

PANAIR DO BRASIL

Unlike Cruzeiro and VARIG, which started with predominantly German-born investors, aircraft, and expertise, Panair do Brasil did so with US support. Originally founded as the New York, Rio, and Buenos Aires Line (NYRBA) on March 17, 1929, it created the operational conditions for a regular air service from Miami, along the South American East Coast to Buenos Aires, and farther over the Andes to Santiago de Chile. The main cargo carried was mail, for which NYRBA had acquired the lucrative licenses of the countries served, with the exception of the United States. On August 21, 1929, the first Sikorsky S-38 flying boat took off from Buenos Aires for its maiden flight to Montevideo. Between February 19 and 25, 1930, the great premiere from Buenos Aires to Miami followed. But NYRBA founder Ralph O'Neil had not reckoned with the charismatic and, at times, ruthless Pan Am founder Juan T. Trippe, who had already secured a commitment from the US Postal Service for the route. O'Neil's airline had thus become worthless, and he had no choice but to transfer NYRBA to Trippe, whose Pan American Airways was officially awarded the mail route by the US government just a few days later. On October 17, 1930, Trippe changed the name of his subsidiary NYRBA do Brasil to Panair do Brasil.

Like Cruzeiro do Sul, Panair do Brasil ordered Caravelle VI-R jets with Rolls-Royce engines and thrust reversers. The four aircraft were received in 1962, and three of them flew in Panair do Brasil colors until the airline's unexpected demise after PP-PDU Antao Leme da Silva had to be taken out of service as a result of structural damage. Due to alleged tax debts, the Brazilian military government revoked the airline's operating license in 1965, without much warning, and transferred the long-haul routes and aircraft to VARIG—while Cruzeiro do Sul was awarded the South American routes. The same year, the Caravelles with the registrations PP-PDV, PP-PDX, and PP-PDZ went to the Brazilian government, which subsequently leased them to Cruzeiro do Sul.

Dramatic takeoff by a Caravelle VI-R of Panair do Brasil, which does not quite comply with today's safety regulations. The temporary subsidiary of Pan American World Airways operated up to four S.E. 210s on its Latin American route network. *Courtesy of Ministério da Defesa / Comando da Aeronáutica / Museu Aeroespacial, Rio de Janeiro*

UNITED AIRLINES

United Airlines' roots go back to Varney Air Lines, founded on April 6, 1926, and Boeing Air Transport, founded by William Boeing in 1927. Always being able to offer the latest aircraft was and is the incentive of the airline group, which merged with Continental Airlines in 2010 to form United Continental Holdings, which since June 2019 has been called United Airlines Holdings.

Thus, in February 1960, United acquired twenty Caravelle VI-Rs as its first jet type for short- and medium-haul flights, which were used to complement its Douglas DC-8s, flown on long-haul routes. The first aircraft was handed over to United on May 31—the last, on July 14, 1961, in Toulouse. On that day, a French national holiday, the first Caravelle delivered by Sud-Aviation and its US partner Douglas Aircraft Company also entered scheduled service with United. The aircraft, intended for the sole North American Caravelle customer, was distinguished by several design changes compared to the other aircraft built. The US certification authority FAA demanded larger cockpit windows for a better external view for the pilots. These large cockpit windows became standard on all subsequent Caravelle versions with Pratt & Whitney engines. United had placed options on a similar number of aircraft, but Sud-Aviation's hopes that these would become firm orders were dashed. Instead of further Caravelles, United turned to the technologically more advanced Boeing 727 and 737. It is interesting that thirteen of the twenty United Caravelles found their way back to Europe and were used by the Danish charter airline Sterling. Its routes included one to the United States from Copenhagen via Gander, Canada, to New York. Other aircraft taken out of service by United remained in the US, such as the Aero Service Caravelle VI-R, also featured in this book.

United brought jet comfort to regional airports in the United States with its twenty Caravelle VI-Rs. *Courtesy of www. aviationancestry.co.uk*

The Caravelle VI-R shown in this press photo published by United Air Lines probably never flew for the American airline. Rather, the aircraft with the factory registration F-WJAP was to be registered as N2001U for United in 1961, but the airline refused to take delivery, for unknown reasons. Instead, it was first used two years later by the Brazilian airline Cruzeiro do Sul with the registration PP-CJC. *Courtesy of Claasen Communication / United Air Lines*

VARIG AND CRUZEIRO DO SUL

Empresa de Viação Aérea Rio Grandense (VARIG) was founded on May 7, 1927, as Brazil's first airline and one of the first airlines worldwide. The airline, founded by the German emigrant Otto Ernst Meyer, took off with the maiden flight of the Dornier do J Wal (Whale) flying boat Atlantico on January 27, 1927, from Rio de Janeiro to Porto Alegre, where it arrived two days later. VARIG quickly established itself as Brazil's flagship, with reliable technology and good service. On the particularly prestigious route to New York, VARIG initially used Lockheed Super Constellation aircraft in the 1950s, and, from December 1959, its first S.E. 210 Caravelle I jets. Among the pilots retrained for the new aircraft type were some older captains whose careers had begun on the Junkers F13 in VARIG's pioneering years. What a difference between the cruising speed of an F13 with a half-open cockpit—87 mph (140 kph)—and the 485 mph (780 kph) of the Caravelle! The pilots were impressed by the S.E. 210's excellent flight characteristics and the low noise levels in the cockpit and cabin. They were particularly enthusiastic about the aircraft's impressive angle of climb after takeoff of up to 25 degrees—and that in a fully loaded aircraft. But the relatively short range of the new jet required four refueling stops on the Porto Alegre–New York route, which opened on December 12, 1959, at the Brazilian cities of Rio de Janeiro and Belem as well as at Port of Spain (Trinidad) and Nassau (Bahamas)—before the "Big Apple" was finally reached after twenty-six tiring hours. This virtually negated the faster jet's time advantage over the piston-engine Super Connic it had replaced. This led to the replacement of the Caravelle on this route by Boeing 707 long-range jets, immediately after the arrival of the first brand-new aircraft, from July 2, 1960. Nevertheless, the two S.E. 210s remained in the VARIG fleet, and another aircraft was ordered after Varig Flight 592-J crashed and burst into flames on September 27, 1961, while on approach to the Brazilian capital of Brasilia. All those on board, including high-ranking government officials, survived, but the S.E. 210 with the registration PP-VJD could not be saved and had to be written off as a total loss. On the other hand, a VARIG Caravelle made aviation history with a record-breaking flight that began on October 11, 1959, over Passo Fundo in southern Brazil. In a glide, the aircraft covered a distance of 203 miles (327 kilometers) in forty minutes from an initial altitude of 39,370 feet (12 kilometers)—with its engines at idle!

The domestic airline Serviços Aéreos Cruzeiro do Sul (Cruzeiro do Sul), which was integrated into VARIG in 1993, no more exists today than the airline into which it was merged after sixty-six years of independence. Cruzeiro do Sul, which was founded in 1933 as a subsidiary of Lufthansa under the name Syndicato Condor Ltda, operated brand-new Caravelle VI-Rs between 1962 and 1975.

For the sake of completeness, it should be mentioned that the Brazilian domestic airline Viação Aérea São Paulo (VASP), founded in 1933, had also placed firm orders for four Caravelle VI-Rs with Rolls-Royce Avon Mk. 533 engines and signed options for two further aircraft. This order never got beyond retouched advertising images of a Caravelle in VASP colors, and none of the aircraft were ever accepted from the manufacturer.

Caravelle

This image is taken from a contemporaneous VARIG advertising brochure and illustrates the use of the Lockheed Super Constellation and the S.E. 210 Caravelle I on the prestigious New York route. *Author's collection Please check photo placement. Nose of Super Constellation to the left is cut off!!!*

The Brazilian airline VASP ordered Caravelle VI-Rs but did not take delivery of any of the machines. Its association with the Caravelle was therefore limited to promotional photos such as this one. *Courtesy of Ministério da Defesa / Comando da Aeronáutica / Museu Aeroespacial, Rio de Janeiro*

The distinctive tail section of a Panair do Brasil Caravelle. *Ministrio da Defesa / Comando da Aeronautica / Museu Aeroespacial, Rio de Janeiro*

CHAPTER 5
INTRODUCING THE CARAVELLE

Swissair took delivery of the factory-new Caravelle III HB-ICU on April 19, 1962. After a little more than eight years, in October 1970, it changed hands and was bought by the French charter airline Catair and registered in France as F-BUFH. *Courtesy of Tom Weihe*

FIRST-FLIGHT ADVENTURES

When an airline opens a new route, it is always a big event. At the gate, a symbolic ribbon is cut by official representatives of the airline and the airport, and those of the two connected cities; photos of the crew are taken on the apron, and the premiere guests are treated to special delicacies and drinks at the gate and on board during the flight. But what happened in Copenhagen on April 26, 1959, was no simple maiden flight, as Scandinavian Airlines had celebrated many times before. After all, the maiden flight of the S.E. 210 Finn Viking from Copenhagen to Beirut was a double world premiere. First, SAS was honored to be the first airline in the world to operate the Caravelle on a scheduled service, ahead of Air France, and second, it was the first-ever scheduled flight by a short-and-medium-haul jet. The previous de Havilland 106 Comet 1, which had been in service for less than two years, had a roughly comparable range, but unlike the Caravelle it had been designed as a long-haul jet for great distances, which it covered with many refueling stops.

In this photo, SAS stewardess Birgitta Lindman is holding the 1958 issue of Life magazine that made her world famous. As the cover girl for a special issue on air travel, Lindman became not only a figurehead for SAS, but also a favorite flight attendant for special flights—such as the two Caravelle premiere flights to Beirut and Cairo in 1959. *Courtesy of SAS*

Alongside Birgitta Lindman, her colleague Carin Ygberg was also responsible for looking after the guests of honor on the two Caravelle premiere flights to Beirut and Cairo. In this photo she is standing on the rear steps of an S.E. 210. *Courtesy of SAS Museum*

SAS sent out invitations, and aviation journalists as well as business partners from all over the world answered the call of the airline's press department. The program included a visit to the cradle of the Caravelle at Sud-Aviation in Toulouse; the Rolls-Royce factories in Derby, England, where the delegation was driven to the factory in a motorcade of fine Rolls-Royce cars; and the source of the delicious meals served on board—the SAS Catering flight kitchen in Copenhagen. The highlight was, of course, a seat on one of the two first flights to Beirut—and a few days later to Cairo. In the cabin, a purser, a steward, and two stewardesses pampered the twenty passengers in first class and fifty in tourist class, which meant that the Caravelle was filled to capacity with invited guests on both premieres. Among them were fifty-three journalists who had traveled from twelve countries to take part in this historic flight to Beirut. Among those looking after them was Birgitta Lindman—the most famous SAS stewardess of that time. She achieved worldwide fame as the cover girl of the American Life magazine in 1958. Lindman beat out competitors from fifty-three other airlines to grace the cover of a special aviation issue of Life. This was a major PR coup for SAS, since in the magazine article Lindman reported extensively on her employer and her not-always-glamorous life as a flight attendant. Together with her colleague Carin Ygberg, also Swedish, Lindman was responsible for looking after the guests of honor on both SAS Caravelle premiere flights. Her duties were not limited to onboard service but also included participation in the extensive sightseeing program at both destinations. While the trip to Beirut included a visit to the ancient archeological sites at Baalbeck and a flight to Jerusalem, the program of the second maiden flight, which took off from Copenhagen for Cairo on May 14, 1959, included the obligatory visit to the pyramids of Giza and the Great Sphinx. As with the trip to Beirut, the aircraft was filled with press representatives from all over the world, who were offered, among other things, a Night in the Orient with culinary delights in addition to a boat trip on the Nile. All in all, the program in Egypt, officially named "Caravelle Press Inauguration Program II," lasted a full seven days!

PROMINENT GUESTS

In the golden age of air transport—from the 1940s to the 1960s—the aircraft was still new as a means of transport, and air fares were so high that most people around the globe could only dream of flying to a faraway destination. Air travel was therefore reserved for "very important people" such as film stars and music legends, representatives of aristocratic houses, and business tycoons. Even high-ranking politicians were regular guests on board scheduled flights in those days. That is scarcely imaginable today, with presidents and ministers mingling with ordinary passengers. At the end of the 1950s, a flight between Germany and New York cost about as much as a brand-new Volkswagen Beetle, for which most Europeans had to save for a long time. So for the majority of people, longing views of the silver birds from airport visitor terraces was all that was within their reach. This was the time before the aircraft hijackings and bombings that shook the aviation industry from the 1970s onward. And so, at some airports, not even a fence separated the action on the apron from the astonished spectators. Flying as a new travel experience also exerted an irresistible fascination on the music and film industries of the 1950s and 1960s. Frank Sinatra's hit song "Come Fly with Me," released in 1958, is still considered a hymn to the dream of flying to distant countries. The original LP cover features an illustration of several Lockheed L-1649A Jetstream propeller planes of Trans World Airlines. The American dream factories in Hollywood also used the very special atmosphere of the airports, propeller-driven airliners, and early jets of the time as exotic backdrops in numerous films. For example, Audrey Hepburn flies across the Atlantic aboard a TWA Lockheed Super Constellation in the 1957 film *Funny Face*, and Carry Grant boards a Northwest Airlines plane in Hitchcock's masterpiece *North by Northwest*.

SAS stewardess Birgitta Lindman looking at the ancient Egyptian inscriptions and wall paintings in Giza. Both Carin Ygberg and Birgitta Lindman had to wear their uniforms during these excursion programs and keep the guests in good spirits. *Courtesy of SAS Museum*

One might think that this photograph was taken as part of the SAS Caravelle premiere to Cairo. But a closer look reveals that it is a photomontage in which the Caravelle prototype 01 F-BHHH was added. *Courtesy of SAS Museum*

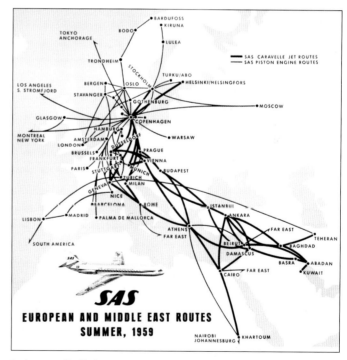

In the second half of 1959, SAS was the airline with the most scheduled jet flights in the world. *Courtesy of SAS Museum*

Arrival of the SAS Caravelle premiere flight in the German metropolis of Düsseldorf on April 26, 1959. Along with Vienna and Athens, it was one of three stops between Copenhagen and Beirut. *Courtesy of Düsseldorf Airport*

Grand reception for the first SAS Caravelle after its landing at the Lebanese capital, Beirut. *Courtesy of SAS Museum*

Interest in the northern European jet visitor was high in Beirut, and a chance to see the inside of the aircraft was highly coveted. *Courtesy of SAS Museum*

Vienna Airport was an important SAS Caravelle hub on the route between northern Europe and the Middle East and North Africa. *Courtesy of Vienna Airport*

The elegance of the Caravelle was also reflected in the uniforms designed by SAS stewardesses. *Courtesy of SAS Museum*

SAS produced painted postcard motifs of its destinations designed in the 1950s and 1960s, such as this motif of the Iraqi capital, Baghdad. A Caravelle destination of the time, as you can easily see from the silhouette of the jet depicted in the image. *Author's collection*

French president Charles de Gaulle during a tour of a newly built SAS Caravelle. *Courtesy of SAS Museum*

Famed jazz trumpeter Louis "Satchmo" Armstrong boards an SAS Caravelle en route to his next performance during a European tour. *Courtesy of Hamburg Airport*

Nikita Khrushchev was the leading statesman of the Soviet Union from 1953 to 1964. The Cuban Missile Crisis took place during his term of office. This photograph shows him in the cockpit of an SAS Caravelle. *Courtesy of SAS Museum*

The special nature of flying at that time was also expressed in the way passengers dressed for their journeys. Suits and ties for the male passengers were just as standard as the ladies' outfits. People "dressed up" for air travel. The airlines met the need to always look one's best during the flight and after landing, with generously dimensioned and equipped washrooms on their aircraft. Here, everything was available that passengers needed to prepare for their radiant appearance on the passenger stairs after a successful landing. Be it for looking into the cameras of the world press, or for the obligatory wave in the direction of waiting friends and relatives.

With the advent of jet air travel in the form of the Caravelle and the first long-haul models—the Comet 4, Boeing 707, and Douglas DC-8, the "jet set" became the epitome of illustrious air travel for the wealthy high society. Today skiing in St. Moritz in the Swiss Alps, tomorrow partying at the Copa Cabana in Rio de Janeiro, and the day after, enjoying a drink on the French Riviera. From then on, the jet allowed anyone who could afford it to become part of a much-admired lifestyle as a citizen of the world.

High society was now joined by playboys and famous artists and writers as part of this new "jet set." And moviegoers dreamed of "jetting" from one adventure to another aboard the fast jets like the world's most famous spy—James Bond, 007.

The new desire to travel, not only that of the "jet set," was supported by the introduction of the cheaper tourist class—including on the Caravelle. While in the 1940s and 1950s it was only the superrich who could afford to fly, the Caravelle made air travel popular. "Flying is for everyone" was the slogan of the German holiday airline LTU, which flew into the jet age with Caravelles and thus to some extent paved the way for today's mass tourism with its S.E. 210s. As did Sterling in Denmark, Sobelair in Belgium, Transavia in Holland, SAM in Italy, and CTA in Switzerland, to name just a few examples of other charter airlines with Caravelle fleets. More and more people could now fulfill their dream of visiting distant lands thanks to lower jet fares, discover and appreciate previously foreign cultures, and make friends between peoples and thus make the world a better place for all the inhabitants of this planet—not least thanks to the S.E. 210!

The world-famous band the Rolling Stones leaving an Air France Caravelle III at Hamburg Airport. *Courtesy of Hamburg Airport*

American jazz pianist, bandleader, and composer Count Basie was among the Caravelle's frequent fliers. *Courtesy of Hamburg Airport*

The Hungarian American actress Zsa Zsa Gabor enjoyed using the fast SAS Caravelle connection between Copenhagen and Vienna. *Courtesy of SAS Museum*

The smile on the face of British pop singer Cliff Richard suggests that he had a pleasant flight on an SAS Caravelle. *Courtesy of Hamburg Airport*

Henry Ford II, grandson of the auto company founder, on his way from Hamburg to Paris in an Air France Caravelle. *Courtesy of Hamburg Airport*

Roger Moore: As debonair in real life as in his role as 007—James Bond. The "jet-set" lifestyle of his on-screen idol was a dream and role model for many of his fans. *Courtesy of Hamburg Airport*

The "Jet Set" à la Caravelle delighted even the smallest passengers. *Courtesy of SAS Museum*

Fleet parade by the West German holiday airline LTU. Four Caravelle 10Rs and two Fokker F28 regional jets are gathered at Düsseldorf Airport in this photo. In the right background, a Sabena Caravelle sneaked into the picture. *Author's collection*

Opposite

Top: The Swiss charter airline CTA offered its Caravelle 10R even in a luxury version with a lounge and beds. Of course, it could also be used in a more austere configuration with ninety-seven seats for the otherwise usual flights to holiday destinations. *Courtesy of Rolf Käufer*

Bottom: Two SAS Caravelles awaiting their planned maintenance checks in the SAS hangars at the former Oslo-Fornebu airport. *Courtesy of SAS Museum*

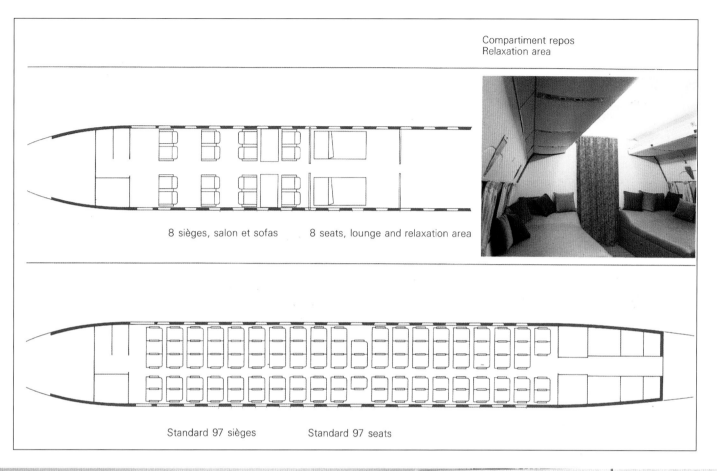

Compartiment repos
Relaxation area

8 sièges, salon et sofas   8 seats, lounge and relaxation area

Standard 97 sièges   Standard 97 seats

Above: The Swiss holiday airline Société Anonyme de Transport Aérien (SATA) began operations in 1966 with Caravelle 10Rs and VI-Rs acquired new and used. Aircraft HB-ICO, pictured here, was an S.E. 210 10R acquired from Sterling Airways. After one of its aircraft crashed off Madeira, SATA was forced to file for bankruptcy in 1978. *Courtesy of Tom Weihe*

Below: Transavia was the only Caravelle operator in the Netherlands. The S.E. 210 III seen here with the registration PH-TRO was originally delivered to Swissair as HB-ICW Solothurn on April 30, 1960. It was, however, owned by SAS. Between 1969 and 1975, it was operated by Transavia and then scrapped in 1976. The nose can be seen in the Dutch aviation museum Aviodrome in Lelystad. *Courtesy of Tom Weihe*

Above: Turn-around of a Finnair Super Caravelle at Copenhagen airport (in those days called Kastrup). *Courtesy of Tom Weihe*

Below: Air France was not the first commercial carrier to operate the S.E. 210. But it was the major international airline to fly it over the longest period of time. *Courtesy of Air France*

CHAPTER 6
IN THE AIR: FLYING THE CARAVELLE

A CARAVELLE CAPTAIN'S PROFESSION OF LOVE

Gunnar Fahlgren was a Caravelle captain from the very beginning. Between 1959 and 1966, he flew the S.E. 210 III on behalf of SAS and its then subsidiary Thai Airways International. He wistfully recalled his time as a Caravelle pilot and dedicated the following declaration of love to it:

Caravelle—yes, the name itself was alluring. It was something of a sensation when SAS announced its order for a large number of these jets in 1957. Earlier aircraft designations usually included the name of the respective manufacturer, such as Douglas, Boeing, or Lockheed, followed by a type number. The Caravelle, however, was a personality in its own right. Right from the start, and without a doubt, it was feminine. Not only its name, but also its shapes and its performance attracted men in droves.

In the 1970s, caricatures of the fleet were printed in the SAS staff magazine *Inside SAS* as introductions to certain chapters, such as this "Caravelle Captain." *Author's collection*

The poem by the Swedish author Nils Ferlin describes the situation at the time very well: "Beauty came to town where cleverness already was." There is no doubt, however, that there was also a certain amount of stupidity among the awakening admirers of that beauty. For example, the practice of flying the long approach from the outer marker of the Instrument Landing System (ILS) at the lowest possible threshold speed frightened us young copilots. We all came to SAS from the Scandinavian air forces and, unlike our captains who were retraining from the airline's propeller-driven aircraft to the Caravelle, had already gained experience on fighter jets. But the reality of life at that time was, unfortunately, that one listened more to rank than to actual experience. The tragic Caravelle accident in January 1960, in which an SAS aircraft crashed on approach to Ankara, could be partly attributed to this nonsensical procedure, which was subsequently abolished.

The fact that flight operations from the short runway of Stockholm's Bromma Municipal Airport went so smoothly was primarily due to the reliability of the Caravelle. We were convinced that an engine failure shortly before reaching V1 would undoubtedly have resulted in a fatal collision between the aircraft and cars on Ulvsundavägen, the road adjacent to the airport. This was despite the theoretical, mathematical calculations of the supervisory gentlemen who wanted to prove the opposite to us pilots. In the course of time, we convinced ourselves that we could trust them.

The Caravelle even had a huge negligee made of nylon. This was in the form of a brake chute that was extended after touchdown and assisted the wheel brakes. The Caravelle III did not have thrust reversers. In the icy Nordic winter, however, it got so cold at the rear that the brake chute housed there often froze. The result was a solid, frozen package that did not deploy but instead rumbled down the runway on a long line behind the Caravelle. Thus her awakening admirers henceforth provided warm air in the tail, whereupon she behaved as expected.

Her power package, in the form of two Rolls-Royce Avon engines, was a revolutionary novelty. Both we as pilots and our passengers loved this engine. For the first time in the history of aviation, it was actually as quiet on board as the airlines' advertising had always promised.

Another great innovation was that the Caravelle no longer had control cables to the control surfaces. Instead, only hydraulic lines were used to transmit the control signals from the cockpit to the surfaces. Many conservative pilots were skeptical and expressed their doubts publicly. I remember that this design initially prevented the Caravelle from being certified in the USA. It was only when Sud-Aviation installed control cables to supplement the hydraulic lines in the aircraft destined for the USA that the Caravelle was also certified on that continent. Perhaps the fatal accident involving a European Swissair Caravelle could have been avoided with these control cables. It went out of control when the hydraulic lines ruptured after a tire explosion and the hydraulic pressure dropped to zero.

She was beautiful to fly! She was beautiful to look at! She glided through the air like a dolphin through water. With the engines switched off, she had a sink rate equivalent to gliders of the time. Because of her clean wings, without slats, she glided smoothly and comfortably to the landing. She flew wherever her nose pointed. Man and airplane formed a natural unit. Her successors, equipped with slats and T-tails, behaved in a completely different way. And numerous accidents with those successors in the 1960s taught pilots to "watch out."

She was beautiful and quiet to fly. Quiet? Yes, for we who sat in the front of the fuselage. But the people living near the airports became increasingly irritated. Especially when the premiere period gave way to everyday life and the Caravelle was forced to work even at night. That it made noise—it couldn't help that. It came onto the market at a time when its buyers thought that noise meant power and not, as today, a waste of energy.

Dear Caravelle! Without a doubt, you have written an important and glorious chapter in aviation history.

Left: A tiger with a human need was the logo of the SAS Caravelle pilots who were members of the "Caramel Club." It was found on the reverse of the ties worn by the pilots. *Courtesy of Gunnar Fahlgren*

Above: This checklist refers to the second prototype, with registration F-BHHI, which was leased by SAS from Sud-Aviation in the first quarter of 1959. This aircraft was used for crew training, among other things. *Courtesy of Gunnar Fahlgren*

Left: This card was issued by SAS and Swissair to help rescue teams to get access to the passenger cabin from the outside in case of an emergency. *Author's collection*

FLYING THE CARAVELLE

Nils Alegren has always had a special fondness for the aircraft from the early days of jet aviation. He spent most of his youth in Toulouse, the heart of European aviation and home of the legendary Caravelle. Even then, he was particularly fascinated by this elegant twin-engine aircraft, on which his mother flew as a stewardess with Air France. When the last Caravelle in Europe was taken out of service at the end of the 1990s, he couldn't shake the idea of buying and restoring a Caravelle cockpit. On his thirtieth birthday, he decided to fulfill all his childhood dreams. Through his internet contacts, he knew exactly where to look to find such a cockpit. His travels took him to Italy, Holland, Thailand, and Cuba. Finally, he got a response from France from the owner of the preferred cockpit—that of an old Air France plane. The idea of building a true-to-the-original flight simulator that would allow the aircraft to be flown and operated in detail convinced the owners, and so he bought the cockpit of the Poitou in September 2012.

In the following four years, he managed to restore the cockpit, putting in five thousand working hours and turning it into a fully functional flight simulator with a modern HD 220° visual display system. One of the highlights during the restoration was definitely the discovery of the boarding pass of Beatle John Lennon. In January 1964, the world-famous band flew from Manchester to Paris on the Poitou, and that boarding pass is from this flight. A forty-year-old chewing-gum wrapper and a gold ring also came to light under the old carpeting.

Nils Alegren, who flies Airbus A330/340 wide-body jets full-time, regrets that it has become increasingly difficult in his day-to-day work as a pilot to bring interested people closer to this fascinating profession. With the commissioning of the simulator, this has changed. Flight enthusiasts can get to know a real flight simulator and pilots at low cost. After fifty-six years, the Poitou took off on its second maiden flight into the virtual sky in May 2016. In May 2020, the simulator was put in storage and moved to Sweden in 2022 where it is being reassembled and made available to the public with updated systems and graphics.

In the following, Nils Alegren describes from the pilot's point of view the differences between the modern Airbus models with fly-by-wire controls that he flies in his daily professional life—and the Caravelle III.

Power plants: The Caravelle III—one of the earlier and most popular versions of the aircraft—was powered by Rolls-Royce Avon Mk. 527 engines producing 51.18 kN (11,505 lbs.) of thrust. For comparison: the most common CFM 56 engine used on A320 series aircraft and Boeing 737 (among many others) has a thrust rating of around 100 kN (22,480 lbs.). Fuel consumption however is approximately 2,400 kg/hr. (5,291 lbs./hr.), which is almost identical to the Caravelle III at high gross weight. The Caravelle III could carry a maximum of ninety-nine passengers, and the Airbus A320 a maximum of 180 passengers.

Today's aircraft are operated extremely efficiently, and that includes very careful engine handling. Wherever possible, a reduced-thrust takeoff is performed. This means the takeoff is accomplished using less thrust than the engines are capable of producing under the existing atmospheric conditions. Additionally, the air-conditioning system is usually switched off for the takeoff run, reducing wear on the engines by bringing the EGT (exhaust gas temperature) down a couple of degrees. EGT is one of the primary parameters of the engines, and the aim is to keep it as low as possible to significantly increase engine life and so-called TBO—time between overhauls. Engine overhauls require that the engine is removed from the aircraft and disassembled, parts inspected and measured, and many parts replaced. It is typically a labor-intensive and hence expensive operation.

There were no reduced-thrust takeoffs on Caravelles powered by the Rolls-Royce Avon. Takeoff power was always at maximum engine thrust at 8,000 rpm, which resulted in greatly reduced engine life and frequent engine changes. Sud-Aviation's 1958 Caravelle Performance Manual states 1,000 hrs. between engine overhauls, which by today's standard of 30,000 hours seems ridiculously low. While the number of hours between overhauls increased through the years to about 4,500 to 5,000, it never reached today's standards.

Flight controls: The Caravelle employed fully powered flight controls. The hydraulic system, which incorporated UK-sourced components, featured four systems—two main systems (Blue and Green) pressurized by the engine-driven hydraulic pumps, and two emergency systems powered by electric pumps (Red and Yellow). Interestingly, Airbus retained the designation of the hydraulic systems until today, and the green system is still the main hydraulic system on the Caravelle and the Airbus A320—and even the A380.

Some of the hydraulic lines of the Caravelle went all the way through the cockpit behind the first officer's seat through the indicators on the overhead panel. It did happen that a leak in the lines resulted in some unpleasant surprises with hydraulic fluid dripping from the panel above the first officer. The electric pump and accumulator for the red hydraulic system was located in the cockpit behind the flight engineer's panel, and its noise was significant and rather distracting.

The rudder, elevators, and ailerons are operated by four servodyne units via a linkage system from the control columns and pedals in the cockpit. Each servodyne unit consisted of two hydraulic actuating cylinders in tandem, with corresponding distributor valve assemblies in the same housing. One of the cylinders in each unit is supplied by the GREEN system, and the other cylinder by the BLUE system. In case of any normal system failure, the YELLOW system acts as an emergency system. Only one cylinder of the servodyne unit is sufficient to provide the correct deflection of the corresponding control surface in any flight condition. There is no mechanical connection between the cockpit controls and the control surfaces. The very same applies to today's Airbus fly-by-wire aircraft, where control inputs are converted into electronic signals and transmitted by wires (hence the term "fly by wire"). The flight control computers then decide how to move the actuators at each control surface to provide the control response. In addition, this concept makes it possible to block, dampen, or add inputs from the pilots. This allows aircraft to automatically trim and limit bank and pitch angles and always remain within the aircraft's design limits. Incidents like the one involving a Caravelle VI-R of Panair do Brasil on September 6, 1963, when a midair collision was avoided by the pilot's extreme flight maneuvers, which damaged the aircraft's structure beyond repair, are a thing of the past with the fly-by-wire system. A large number of Caravelle accidents were attributed to CFIT, or controlled flight into terrain, due to lack of situational awareness and poor equipment. Today's EGPWS, or enhanced ground-proximity warning systems, compare the aircraft's location and topographic data obtained from satellites, and warn the pilot of danger if the aircraft is flying into a mountain (however, not necessarily man-made objects). An immediate escape maneuver can be flown with full aft stick and full power up to 2.5 g without fears of damaging the aircraft's structure. The climb rates achieved can be overwhelming, however.

The nose section of the Poitou, sister aircraft of the Auvergne shown here, is the basis for the S.E. 210 flight simulator built by Nils Alegren in around five thousand hours of work. *Courtesy of Tom Weihe*

Cockpit ergonomics: Entering a Caravelle cockpit is literally a step back in time and feels more like entering a spaceship from a very old science-fiction story. The cockpit is cramped and is lower than the cabin floor for increased space and comprises four seats for two pilots, a flight engineer, and an observer seat, now commonly called the jump seat. The similarity to the de Havilland Comet is immediately evident, even though the cockpit section was eventually completely redesigned and reinforced by Sud-Aviation after the Comet accidents. The basic layout of the pilot's panel includes the basic T instrument arrangement, and pilots become comfortable in the cockpit after a relatively short time. Interestingly, the basic T arrangement, with the artificial horizon, airspeed indicator on the left, compass below, and altimeter to the right, remains the same on the Airbus, albeit displayed on screens with some additional information.

The Caravelle III was operated with a flight engineer by most airlines. There was no technical reason to have a flight engineer, but many unions insisted on operating the Caravelle with a three-man flight deck. Sabena modified some of its Caravelles to a two-man flight deck, and later models were operated with just two pilots. Finnair and Austrian always operated with two pilots only.

Engine instrumentation is very basic, with gauges displaying rpm, EGT (exhaust gas temperature), fuel flow rate, oil pressure, and engine temperatures. A very famous instrument on the early Caravelle was the fuel-used indicator, which clicked with every kilogram of fuel burned, and many pilots remember the very distinctive clicking. A feature that stands out is the "low-pressure fuel levers" next to the thrust levers. These are used only in case of engine failure and were lock-wired in the forward position. Fuel levers and thrust levers were incorporated into the same levers. This led to several mishaps, with engines being shut down accidentally in flight, and they were changed on later models. Unusual for today's jet pilots is the lack of thrust reversers and spoilers. Though speed brakes are installed, they do not have the same effect as spoilers since they are mounted on the top and bottom of the wing and are fantastic devices for deceleration at high speeds, but not for destroying lift on the upper surface of the wing and increasing brake efficiency. Later Caravelle models were fitted with thrust reversers and spoilers for better landing performance. The Caravelle III and VI-N featured a brake chute—used only in an emergency or when landing on short runways. It was deployed on touchdown, and it was not released until the aircraft reached its parking position. It then had to be packed into its container again by maintenance personnel, while a spare container was usually installed for the return flight.

Air France operated the Caravelle with two ADFs, two VORs, and one DME only. There were four radio magnetic indicators for VOR and NDB navigation, and two PDIs (pictorial deviation indicators) used for ILS and VOR interception, and one DME indicator on the captain's side. Very basic by today's standard. Early versions of the Caravelle were certified to CAT 1 operations only, with 800 meters (2,625 ft.) visibility. Today, Autoland is one of the key elements enabling standard and reliable flight operations, even in low-visibility conditions down to CAT 3b (runway visual range of 75 meters or 250 ft.).

Interestingly, it was the Caravelle that paved the way to automatic approaches and landings, and on January 9, 1969, the first-ever fully automatic landing by a commercial aircraft with passengers was performed by an Air Inter Caravelle III at Paris-Orly.

Impressions of the Caravelle simulator originally set up at the gates of the southern German metropolis of Munich and moved to Sweden in 2022. *Courtesy of www.flycaravelle.com*

The Caravelle III of the Le Caravelle Club in Stockholm-Arlanda is no longer airworthy, but in the summer of 2021 it started its engines again for a "tour" of the airport. Nils Alegren was in the captain's seat. *Courtesy of Nils Alegren*

Rolf Käufer and his son Christian—founder and current managing director of the TFC pilot-training center in Essen, together with son Bernt Käufer, gained extensive Caravelle flying experience at LTU, SAT, and Aero Lloyd. *Courtesy of Christian Käufer, www.tfc-kaeufer.de*

Procedures: The operating procedures differ significantly from today's standard. It starts off with the tiller, the small wheel on the captain's control column for steering the aircraft on the ground. Only the captain was able to taxi the airplane. Today's Airbus cockpit layout and procedures allow both the captain and first officer to taxi the aircraft, depending on their roles as pilot monitoring or pilot flying. Both pilots have a tiller next to the side stick.

After the first engine start, 10 degrees of flap would be selected, and after landing, flaps would be retracted to 10 degrees until reaching parking position to avoid foreign object damage. You will hardly ever see a video or photo of a Caravelle taxiing with flaps retracted.

Standing takeoff was standard operating procedure on the Caravelle. Full power was applied while holding the brakes until both engines were stabilized at takeoff rpm. This procedure is no longer used today, when commonly the brakes are released at 50 percent engine thrust to avoid engine damage from objects or gravel on the runway. A major difference is the chrono used for acceleration. The time to accelerate to 100 kts was calculated during cockpit preparation and was an additional safety feature to confirm adequate acceleration and correct thrust setting.

Climb-out was very different on the Caravelle. Acceleration to 250 kts had priority over gaining altitude: SOP (standard operating procedure) was to climb at 1,000 fpm until reaching 250 kts, after which climb would continue at that speed to FL100, where 280 kts or more was usually flown. This gave the Caravelle very shallow climb angles, and noise concerns were not yet an issue. Soon, however, some airports implemented noise abatement procedures, which were flown at V2 + 15kts until 80 seconds after brake release (800 feet minimum), when the nose was lowered and power reduced from 8,100 rpm to 7,350 rpm and climb continued at V2+25 and minimum climb rate of 500 fpm. Upon reaching 2,000 ft., power was increased to standard climb power of 7,700 rpm.

The Caravelle's excellent gliding capabilities can be challenging when speed and altitude need to be reduced quickly. The speed brakes, mentioned earlier, were very effective in killing lift and increasing drag. At high speeds, however, vibration was significant, and Air France recommended turning on the "Fasten seat belt" signs prior to extending the speed brakes at high speed.

Father and son Christian before the next flight in an SAT S.E. 210 Caravelle 10 R. *Courtesy of Christian Käufer, www.tfc-kaeufer.de*

CHAPTER 7
IN THE AIR: THE PASSENGER'S FAVORITE

Boarding an SAS Caravelle over the red carpet. In the "golden age of air transport," the passenger was literally queen or king. *Courtesy of SAS Museum*

In the early years of Caravelle operations, the customer was king—at least for most of the airlines united in the International Air Transport Association, the IATA. As the subsequent history of the world airline association shows, the only way to survive in the competition between the—for the most part—state-owned airlines was to shine with outstanding service, and thus to retain passengers. The example of Erik Ejsenhardt, the long-serving SAS chief pastry chef, who was responsible for the desserts served on board the airline's aircraft for more than thirty-five years, shows the stylistic bloopers that this sometimes led to. When the SAS chef decided to offer a dessert for first-class passengers, with cloudberries as the main ingredient, Ejsenhardt bought 3 tons of them! Every single cloudberry picked in Scandinavia that season went into Ejsenhardt's dessert creations above the clouds! Since those pioneering days, the airline world has undoubtedly changed drastically. IATA has largely lost its regulatory role with the liberalization of air transport, not only in the United States and Europe. Nowadays, it sees itself in a leading role when it comes to global standards in e-ticketing, defense against terrorism in air transport, and the globally increasingly important issue of the ecological compatibility of air travel, new topics that reflect the zeitgeist of the twenty-first century.

IATA: THE GLOBAL COMPETITION CARTEL IN THE CARAVELLE ERA

The first airline association by this name dates back to August 28, 1919, when Det Danske Luftfartselskab (DDL), Deutsche Luftreederei (DLR), Britain's Air Transport and Travel Ltd, Norway's Det Norske Luftfartsrederi (DNL), and Sweden's Svenska Lufttrafik Aktiebolaget founded the first airline umbrella organisation called IATA. Only a few months old themselves, they quickly recognised the need to establish common ground for regulated, cross-border airline operations. Ten years after its foundation, the pre-war IATA already had twenty-three members, all based in Europe. It was not until the 1930s that the network of IATA carriers expanded around the globe, gaining a prominent global player in Pan American Airways. In addition to standardising documents such as tickets and air waybills, IATA members also agreed on common flight operation standards, legal issues, and contacts with authorities and government organisations. At that time, the aircraft was a completely new means of transport for which there were no internationally binding regulations. Thus, the IATA Technical Committee contributed to such fundamental things as the clockwise direction of rotation of cockpit displays, which is still valid today. Or a uniform forward movement of the throttles to increase engine power. Even the seating arrangement in the cockpit—captain on the left, co-pilot on the right—was universally established by IATA at the time, and is taken for granted today.

The outbreak of the Second World War brought civil air traffic around the globe to an almost complete standstill. Thus, the first IATA also perished in the turmoil of war. Nevertheless, representatives of thirty-five airlines from North and South America, Europe, Asia, and Australia met in Chicago in December 1944, while the war was still raging, to set the first course for post-war air transport. The airlines' opinion was urgently needed, as that same year government representatives from the Allied and neutral states had founded the International Civil Aviation Organization (ICAO) as a branch of the United Nations. While ICAO continues to set the global standards for safe and orderly air transport to this day, the "new" IATA, founded in Havana, Cuba[,] in 1945, is closely involved with the implementation of these standards as the world umbrella organisation for airlines. In its founding preamble, IATA set itself the goals, among others, of promoting safe, regular[,] and economical air transport for the benefit of the world's population, to identify methods of cooperation between the companies involved in air transport[,] and, finally, to cooperate closely with ICAO and other international organisations.

One of IATA's focal points is the "Clearing House," opened in 1947, with the help of which airlines can settle their mutual financial claims. IATA increasingly developed into a global cartel in which, with the approval of the governments involved, all details of the flights offered between two countries were agreed, including the air fares, which were identical and binding for all participants. Competition on ticket prices was thus completely eliminated until the gradual liberalisation of air transport, which began in the United States in 1978.

The basis for the global IATA cartel was laid in 1946 by Great Britain and the United States. Their government representatives met in January of that year on the British island of Bermuda to negotiate a compromise regarding the two governments' differing views on fair competition in transatlantic air transport. Even before the Second World War, the USA had stipulated that airlines should operate exclusively with private capital and according to economic principles. This was different than in most nations around the globe, including Britain. The British Overseas Airways Corporation (BOAC), which specialised in long-haul flights, was wholly state-owned, as were most other Western European airlines. Therefore, British negotiators demanded a level of regulation that would protect the interests of both countries involved. The result of the negotiations was the

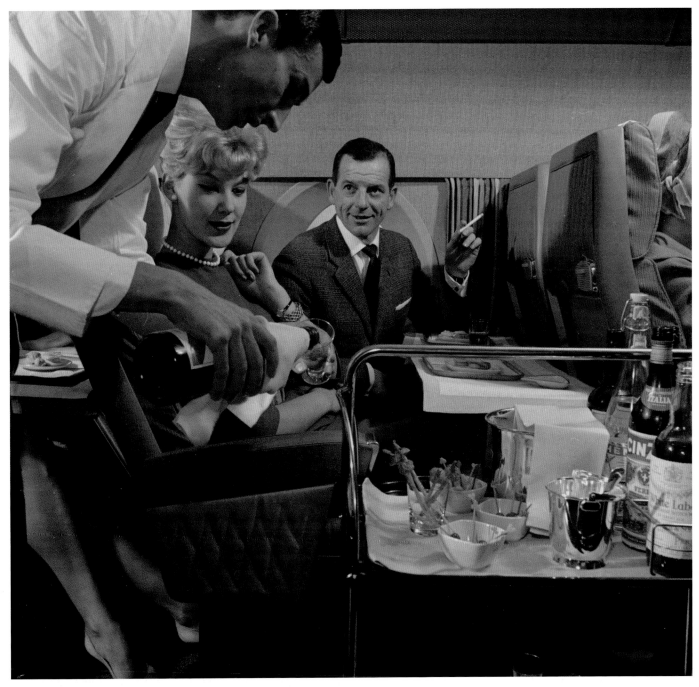

Passengers were pampered with exquisite food and drink both in first and tourist classes in the nascent Caravelle era. And that even on short- and medium-haul routes. *Courtesy of ETH-Bibliothek Zürich, Bildarchiv / Stiftung Luftbild Schweiz / photographer: Swissair / LBS_SR03-20444 / CC BY-SA 4.0*

"Bermuda Agreement." It stated that the governments of the USA and Great Britain would jointly determine which airlines would be allowed to fly on individual routes and at what capacity. The selected airline also had to be predominantly owned by institutions or individuals based in the airline's home country. In order to make the offer one hundred percent transparent, it was also agreed to set a uniform airfare, the negotiation of which was entrusted to IATA. The example was set and soon the regional IATA transport conferences established universally applicable standards for international routes around the globe. This applied not only to ticket prices, but also to ticket formats, handling procedures, technical standards on the ground and in the air, as well as accounting among the airlines. The biggest advantage for the passenger was the transparency of air fares and the possibility to travel on one ticket with several airlines at identical fares.

In 1951, American Airlines raised the idea of a second class, called Tourist Class, at an IATA conference in Nice, France. Until then, there had only been a very expensive First Class on board scheduled flights. The idea did not meet with the approval of all airlines, some of which feared for their income. But eventually all IATA members agreed on a ticket price for the new booking class that would be about a third lower than that of First Class. In May 1952, the new travel class was introduced with great success, initially on routes across the North Atlantic. Passenger numbers increased to such an extent that IATA authorised its members to introduce Tourist Class on European routes and on flights to the Middle East from April 1, 1953. As much as price-fixing among airlines was criticised even then, the technological standardisation among IATA carriers was advantageous. For example, a phone call to an airline was sufficient to book seats for flights with various airlines on one ticket. This was particularly advantageous as only a few airlines offered daily connections on long-haul routes. Only in combination with the routes of several airlines was a relatively dense route network available to travellers at the time. To a certain extent, the IATA cartel anticipated what the individual airline alliances, such as Star Alliance or Skyteam, are living up to today.

Being pampered with outstanding service on the ground and on board was a special experience for Caravelle passengers in those IATA cartel years. Brazil's VARIG certainly offered by far the most comfortable way to travel. On its twenty-six-hour flight from Porto Alegre to New York, which premiered on October 2, 1959, the Caravelle I was equipped with forty first-class seats. There were ten rows of seats, with two generously proportioned seats on each side of the aisle. The reason for this generous cabin layout was not so much the comfort aspect, but the limited range of the Caravelle I. The number of passengers and the number of available seats were limited. With a larger number of passengers and their luggage, even the four stopovers required for refueling would not have been sufficient on this prestigious route. No wonder that the two Caravelles were quickly replaced by the first Boeing 707s arriving at VARIG in the summer of 1960. Immediately after their replacement on the New York route, the aircraft were gradually given less and less comfortable seating, first with fifty-two, then sixty-eight, and finally seventy-three seats, to serve domestic and South American routes.

Completely independent of the airline and booking class, however, was the general flying experience on board an S.E. 210. Time and again, contemporaneous reports emphasized as a particular highlight the quietness in the passenger cabin, hitherto unknown in air travel, as well as the absence of vibration caused by piston engines. What airlines had promised in their advertising for other aircraft types before the Caravelle entered scheduled service, but could not deliver, had now actually become reality—the guests literally floated above the clouds and hardly noticed the changing attitude of the aircraft. It was the same for the cabin crew, who also had to get used to the new Caravelle feeling. It could happen that the crew in the front galley was so busy pouring the welcome champagne that they noticed the aircraft taking off only when they looked out of the window. It was not quite so quiet in the rear of the S.E. 210, where the two Rolls-Royce or Pratt & Whitney engines were clearly audible in the last rows of seats, the rear galley, and the two washrooms.

But let's let an unnamed journalist from the Deutsche Verkehrs Zeitung and their personal impressions of their flight aboard a Caravelle in 1961 speak for themselves:

Since SAS operates its international network, apart from domestic traffic, almost exclusively with jets, we find a Caravelle at Gate 12 ready to board. What was a sensation yesterday has become a matter of course today. Three years ago still a much-publicized wonder bird, the ingenious design from French aircraft makers has long since become a reliable workhorse in the medium-haul sector. When SAS decided at the time to select this new type with the turbines at the rear of the fuselage for its jet fleet, it may have been considered a bold pioneering act, but in the meantime even the Americans have added Caravelles to their fleets. Perhaps it is precisely this development that shows that those in charge of the Scandinavian company at the time had a very fine nose for the promising technical developments of the future. Even more than its operational performance record, the popularity it managed to gain among travelers speaks highly for this aircraft type.

"You can now see Belgrade, the capital of Yugoslavia, to your left," the captain's course announcement interrupts the soft radio music. Once again we have flown over a national border. Almost silently, our "magic carpet" carries us across countries and seas. Again and again it is impressive how little the passenger in the Caravelle feels the work of the turbines, which push the 43-ton bird forward with 5,000 kg (11,023 lbs. of thrust) each. The soothing silence in the cabin may really become apparent only when one has to continue one's journey in conventional propeller-type equipment. Then the progress that has been made reveals itself, not only allowing one to fly faster, but also more pleasantly and comfortably. But this is precisely what—as experience teaches—is increasingly appreciated, because speed is now a matter of course in air transport and is no longer a selling point.

SAS and Swissair took care to install spacious galleys capable of accommodating the large quantities of food and drink required for the various flight legs. *Courtesy of ETH-Bibliothek Zurich, Bildarchiv / Stiftung Luftbild Schweiz / photographer: Swissair / LBS_SR03-20441 / CC BY-SA 4.0*

Juliette Gréco (1927–2020), French actress and singer, known as "la grande dame de la chanson," was a frequent Caravelle VIP traveler. *Hamburg Airport*

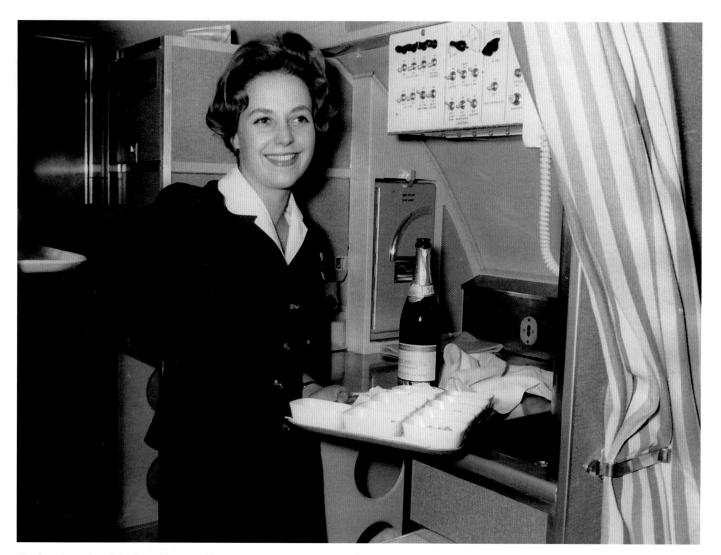

Good service on board the Caravelle came with a smile, as demonstrated here by flight attendant Jeannette Schlossmacher on the maiden flight of the Austrian Airlines S.E. 210 in 1963. *Courtesy of Austrian Airlines*

Meeting of two aircraft generations. A Douglas DC-3 of the Yugoslavian airline JAT from the 1930s and a then-ultra-modern Caravelle of Austrian Airlines. *Courtesy of Austrian Airlines*

A flight on the Caravelle was a fascinating experience for all three genera-tions. *Courtesy SAS Museum*

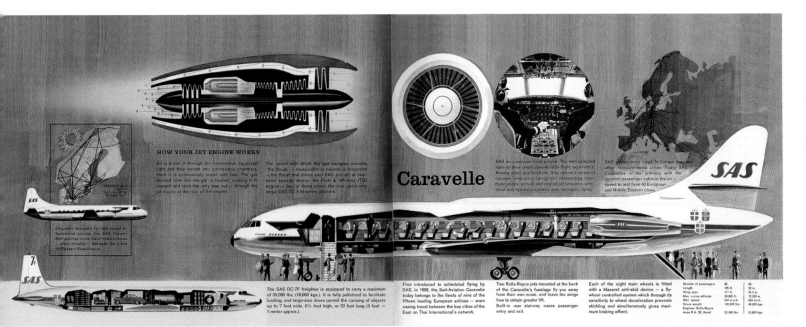

This cutaway drawing of an SAS Caravelle is taken from one of the airline's contemporaneous brochures. There is also an explanation of the functioning of a jet engine and a short type history of the SAS Douglas DC-7 freighters and the Convair 440 used on shorter routes. *Author's collection*

Traveling well dressed, and not only on board a Swissair Caravelle, was fashionable in the 1960s. *Courtesy of ETH-Bibliothek Zurich, Bildarchiv / Stiftung Luftbild Schweiz / photographer: Swissair / LBS_SR03-20443 / CC BY-SA 4.*

Long before the introduction of screens above the seats, or even at every single seat, slips of paper on which the captain had noted down information about the flight's progress were passed through the cabin from one row of passengers to the next. *Courtesy of Gunnar Fahlgren*

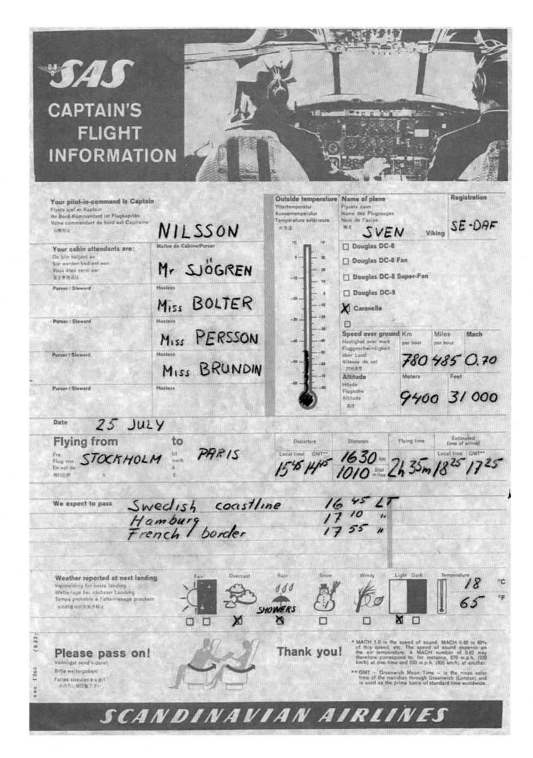

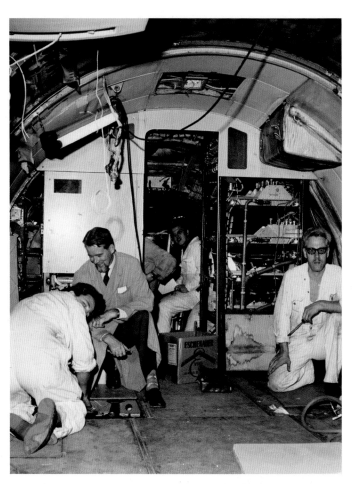

The landing gear of the S.E. 210 was designed to allow supersmooth landings. In addition to the very smooth flight and the silence in the passenger cabin, this was a feature of the Caravelle welcomed by all passengers. *Courtesy of SAS Museum*

During a so-called D-check, each and every component as well as the structure are thoroughly checked by the aircraft technicians. Here a SAS Caravelle at the so called Linta workshops of the airline, located at the Swedish capital city of Stockholm. *SAS Museum*

After the oil price shock of the early 1970s, the passenger cabins of many Caravelles on the main air routes were converted to higher-density seating, and first class was abolished. The result was a tourist-only class on SAS as well, which remained standard until the type was retired in 1974. *Author's photo*

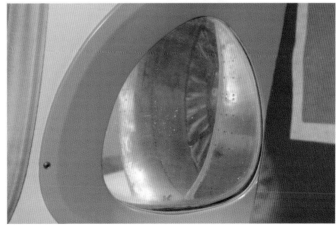

The view through the Caravelle III triangle shaped cabin window on to a Rolls-Royce Avon engine. *Author's collection*

CHAPTER 8
CARAVELLE TALES

Above and opposite: In addition to numerous Caravelles, the French domestic carrier Air Inter was also the sole user of the Dassault Mercure. Over the decades, not a single one of the airline's passenger was injured in either type of aircraft. *Courtesy of Tom Weihe and author's collection*

Avec les compliments d'Air Inter

AIR INTER

on utilise mieux Air Inter quand on choisit bien ses horaires

JET RECIPES FOR HOME COOKING

Following the maxim "One should eat in order to live, not live in order to eat," by the French writer Molière (1622–1673), in 1959 the Scandinavian airline SAS launched a very special cookbook. SAS Jetline Recipes contained recipes for twelve dishes served exclusively on board their Caravelle jetliners. The Scandinavians were so proud of their hot and cold gastronomic creations for the physical well-being of passengers on board their new jetliner that they had this small cookbook printed, so that their passengers could re-create the dishes served above the clouds in their own kitchens. The recipe book included creations, shown here, with imaginative names such as "Cold Fillets Mignon Caravelle," "Jet Brioche," or "Poached Eggs SAS Style" and provided an exact list of ingredients and cooking instructions for home use, including a color photo as a serving suggestion.

SAS left nothing to chance in terms of what was served in the air on board the new jets, and developed a new kitchen concept called Caravelle Cuisine especially for the S.E. 210. To realize this, every kitchen material, every spoon, and every plate was specially designed for the Caravelle flights in the airline's own experimental flight kitchen in Stockholm, and every recipe was continually refined. Also completely new were the electric kitchens installed on the S.E. 210 aircraft, which could bring meals prepared on the ground to the desired serving temperature within twenty seconds. To ensure that nothing was left to chance, SAS also tested these kitchens extensively in advance and optimized the meals for this then completely new but now-standard method of in-flight catering. Even the speed of the coffee machine, which had been specially developed for the Caravelle, was adapted to the shorter flight times of the new jets. It was now able to produce twelve freshly brewed cups of coffee in three minutes, instead of making the coffee on the ground beforehand and merely keeping it warm in the air, as had been the case in the previous propeller age.

The menus presented to passengers on all Caravelle flights contained a suggested menu for each leg of the journey, but guests were free to choose from any of the dishes available on each "leg" between the departure airport of Copenhagen and the final destination in Africa or the Middle East. And there were plenty of these stops. After all, the flight time was rarely more than an hour between the numerous stopovers on the way from northern Europe to Greece, Turkey, Egypt, Sudan, Lebanon, Syria, Iraq, or Iran. Further stops were made in between, depending on the flight number, in Germany, Austria, Czechoslovakia, or Hungary. Flights from Copenhagen to Cairo, for example, made three stops en route, and other routes started from the Danish capital and went as far as the Iranian metropolis of Tehran in the east and the Sudanese city of Khartoum in the south. Looking at the menu sequence shown on flight SK 874 from Cairo to Copenhagen, it quickly becomes clear that no passenger left hungry. Readers of this book can be assured that this was the catering offered in economy class on a medium-haul flight—which, moreover, was included in the fare!

In the SAS Caravelle age, these kind of tags were attached to the cabin baggage. *Author's collection*

SAS distributed the booklet "Jetline Recipes" on its aircraft and in travel agencies, as well as to good customers. It contained recipes for dishes served on board the airline's Caravelle fleet. They were intended to motivate people to cook the dishes at home and thus to develop a new desire to fly on an SAS Caravelle. *Author's collection*

1 BRIOCHE A LA JET
Jet Brioche

for 5 persons

10 brioches
4 small sweetbreads, skinned and cleaned
1 cup mushrooms
1 tablespoon pâté de foie gras
1 cup thick cream
1 tablespoon flour
2 tablespoons butter
1 small glass Sherry
Salt, pepper, shallots, Epice Riche

A hollowed, well heated brioche, filled with blanched sweetbreads, mushrooms and pâté de foie gras.

Blanch the sweetbreads and boil slowly for 10 minutes in lightly salted water to which one shallot and a dash of pepper have been added.

Dice the sweetbreads and mushrooms, dust with flour, season with salt and pepper and fry in butter together with finely chopped shallots. Add Sherry, cover and let simmer for 10 minutes. Finally, add the cream, pâté de foie gras and Epice Riche just before filling the heated brioches.

6 MIGNONETTES CARAVELLES
Cold Fillets Mignon "Caravelle"

for 4 persons

4 Fillets Mignon, (appr. 60 gr. (2 oz) each)
4 slices white bread, toasted
8 artichoke-bottoms Italian type
8 small slices pâté de foie gras

For Salad
1 head lettuce
Oil dressing
Lemon juice
Salt and pepper

Fried Fillets Mignon served cold on toast with Italian artichoke-bottoms topped with a slice of pâté de foie gras. Serve the salad as a side dish, but flavour the dressing with lemon juice instead of vinaigrette in order to retain the full piquancy of the pâté de foie gras taste.

11 CREPES AUX MORILLES
French Pancakes with Creamed Morels

for 6 persons

4 cups pancake batter (12 "crepes")

Sauce
2 cups morels
½ onion
2 tablespoons butter
2 cups thick cream
White wine, salt, pepper

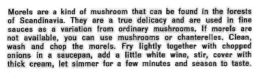

Morels are a kind of mushroom that can be found in the forests of Scandinavia. They are a true delicacy and are used in fine sauces as a variation from ordinary mushrooms. If morels are not available, you can use mushrooms or chanterelles. Clean, wash and chop the morels. Fry lightly together with chopped onions in a saucepan, add a little white wine, stir, cover with thick cream, let simmer for a few minutes and season to taste.

Fry small pancakes, pour the creamed morels over the pancakes, roll them up and place them side by side in a casserole or baking dish. Sprinkle with grated cheese and melted butter and bake in a hot oven. Serve straight from the oven in the casserole.

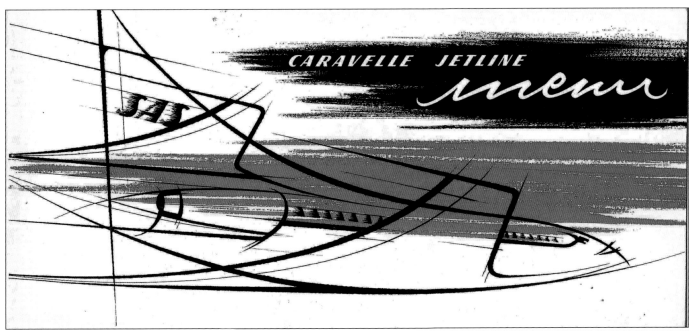

On board the SAS Caravelles, stewardesses passed out not only the recipe book but also the menus for the various flight segments. Here as an example, from flight SK 874 from Cairo, via Athens, Budapest, and Düsseldorf to Copenhagen. *Author's collection*

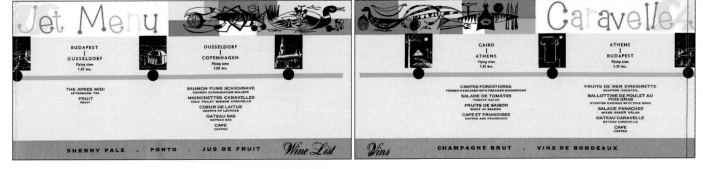

The following article (*opposite page*) from a South German regional newspaper from January 1961 describes the service provided on board an SAS Caravelle on the flight between Stuttgart and Madrid. SAS flew its S.E. 210s from Stuttgart, the headquarters of the world-famous car manufacturers Mercedes and Porsche, from the 1959–60 winter schedule until the summer of 1968. Domestic destinations were Frankfurt and Munich, as well as Gothenburg (Göteborg), Copenhagen, Oslo, and Stockholm in Scandinavia; Barcelona, Lisbon, and Madrid on the Iberian Peninsula; and Nice on the French Riviera. This was made possible by extensive traffic rights granted to SAS by the Western Allies for their occupation zones immediately after the end of the Second World War. Until the new Lufthansa began operations on April 1, 1955, SAS took on the role of the West German "national carrier" on a proxy basis. Its dense domestic German route network and the European and intercontinental routes offered from Germany literally gave wings to the German economic miracle of the 1950s. Even after the 1955 return of air sovereignty to the Federal Republic of Germany, which had been founded six years earlier, SAS initially invoked its traditional flight rights. But in the second half of the 1950s, the then West German

Copenhagen—Dusseldorf
1 hr.*

"SMØRREBRØD" DE LUXE DANOIS
De Luxe Danish Open Sandwiches

CAFE ET PETITS FOURS
Coffee and Petits Fours

Dusseldorf—Vienna
1 hr. 20 mins.*

SAUMON FROID PARISIENNE
Cold Salmon Parisienne

COTELETTE DE POULET VIENNOISE
Fried Chicken Viennese Style
SAUCE CHASSEUR
Chasseur Sauce
POMMES FONDANTES
Roast Potatoes
PETITS POIS FRANÇAISE
Green Peas Française

POIRE BELLE HELENE
Belle Helene Pear

MOCCA
Mocha

Vienna—Istanbul
2 hrs. 5 mins.*

DOBOS SCHNITTE
BISCUIT MADELEINE

FRUITS DE SAISON
Selected Fresh Fruit

CAFE OU THE
Coffee or Tea

FOR PASSENGERS FROM VIENNA:

Also
DELICE DE TARTINE SUEDOISE
Swedish Combination Sandwich

vins

VINS BLANCS

CHAMPAGNE BRUT
Moët et Chandon Impérial

BORDEAUX
Graves Rosechatel

VINS ROUGES

BORDEAUX
Château Smith-Haut-Lafitte
BOURGOGNE
Gevrey-Chambertin

XERES
Sherry Pale Tio Pepe

Istanbul—Beirut
1 hr. 30 mins.*

SALADE DE HOMARD
Lobster Salad

FILET MIGNON BORDELAISE
Fillet Mignon Bordelaise
POMMES NOISETTE
Noisette Potatoes
HARICOTS VERTS AU BEURRE
Buttered String Beans
TOMATE FARCIE
Stuffed Tomato

PLATEAU DE FROMAGES
Cheese Tray

FLAN PARISIENNE
French Apple Pie

MOCCA
Mocha

Beirut—Damascus
20 mins.*

APERITIFS
Drinks

Damascus—Cairo
1 hr. 10 mins.*

"SMØRREBRØD" DE LUXE DANOIS
De Luxe Danish Open Sandwiches

CAFE ET PETITS FOURS
Coffee and Petits Fours

* Time quoted = air-borne time

transport minister Hans-Christoph Seebohm pushed for a gradual withdrawal of SAS from Germany. This was done to benefit the new Lufthansa. This step was finally taken at the beginning of the 1960s. By then, SAS had gradually left most of the intercontinental routes from West Germany, such as New York, Johannesburg, Khartoum, Recife, Rio de Janeiro, Montevideo, Buenos Aires, Santiago de Chile, Karachi, Calcutta, Rangoon, Bangkok, Hong Kong, Manila, and Tokyo, as well as the domestic German and European connections to Lufthansa, and established a neighborly traffic partnership with Lufthansa between Scandinavia and Germany. Until the 1970s, however, the flying Scandinavians continued to offer European and intercontinental destinations from Germany. For example, SAS Douglas DC-9s flew from Copenhagen via Stuttgart to Athens, Cairo, and Madrid, and DC-8s from Düsseldorf to Lagos.

Filet à la Caravelle—Eaten over Cannes, but the food is prepared in Echterdingen.

The Scandinavian airline is the only one to maintain its own galley at Stuttgart Airport. When its route network was expanded, the kitchen was set up in Echterdingen in February 1959. Today, two cooks and female helpers are busy here preparing the meals that are intended to make the journey pleasantly shorter for passengers on their way south or to Scandinavia. The feasting begins shortly after takeoff from Echterdingen. "The apres midi—afternoon tea" is what it says on every passenger's menu card, on which the menu for the entire flight is listed. The stewardess serves a variety of sandwiches, tea, several kinds of pastries, and fresh fruit. The flight from the Filder Plain to the Riviera takes one hour and five minutes.

The next "hop" is to Madrid. Flight time one hour and forty-five minutes. So you have plenty of time to eat a hearty meal. The cooks in Echterdingen have prepared it ready to go, and now it just needs to be quickly heated up again on board. That takes all of three or four minutes in the electric cooker. "Smoked Scandinavian salmon, roasted duckling bigarade, mixed salads, mocha solaire, coffees," we read on the menu.

Generally, the menus change every four weeks. Currently, for example, on the Stuttgart–Madrid route, beef fillet in herb butter is served toward evening, along with young green beans, nut potatoes, and a stuffed tomato. Usually, the menus are worked out in the central kitchen in Stockholm according to the season, and the individual galleys—the airline has four such facilities in Germany—then prepare the meals. "But we can also make our own suggestions," says the chef in Echterdingen. The food is bought in Stuttgart shops; all vegetables and fruit are purchased at the Stuttgart wholesale market. In addition, Echterdingen has its own bonded warehouse with spirits, cigarettes, and perfumes that are sold on board the aircraft.

The jet age has also presented the catering industry with new challenges. Whereas it used to take two hours to get from one place to another, today the time has shrunk by half. These shortened flight times mean that the menu has also had to be changed. SAS, for example, has created twenty "Caravelle–Jetline–Menus," the recipes for which passengers can even take with them if they wish, so that the lady of the house can braise such a "Caravelle jet fillet" herself on the cooker at home.

At present, the cooks in Echterdingen produce around 1,100 complete meals every month. Last summer it was up to nearly 2,000 meals. (*Esslinger Zeitung*, January 1961)

First air mail letter carried on the first SAS Caravelle flight on July 23, 1959, from Stuttgart to Copenhagen. *Author's collection*

The income generated by the transport of air cargo contributes now and then a lot to the commercial success of a specific air route. *SAS Museum*

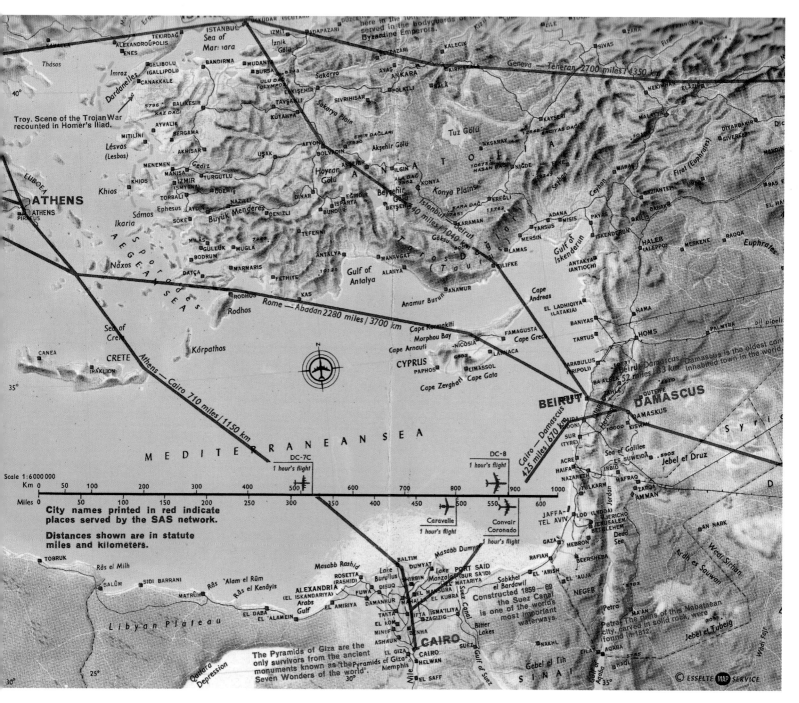

This segment of an SAS route map from the early 1960s clearly shows the different distances covered by a propeller-driven aircraft in one flying hour, in direct comparison with the first jets, such as the Caravelle, Douglas DC-8, and Convair 990 Coronado. *Author's collection*

Of course, SAS was not the only airline to pamper its guests on Caravelle flights from the very beginning. The S.E. 210 fleet operated by its partner airline Swissair, of which the first four of a total of nine aircraft were leased by SAS until Swissair acquired them from its northern European partner in 1965, had an identical cabin and galley layout. The legendary Swissair service was, of course, also offered in first and tourist class on board its Caravelles. For many decades, the Swiss carrier was synonymous with outstanding customer service and excellent marketing and was thus an international flagship for Switzerland. The beauty of the Swiss mountain scenery—but above all the Swiss banking secrecy of the time—led to a stream of well-heeled first-class passengers traveling to the Swiss financial centers, which kept the airline's coffers well filled over a long period of time. The airline's employees were so proud of their employer that it was not uncommon for them to have themselves listed in the local telephone directory as "Swissair employee(s)" at their own request.

Swissair, traditionally known for its excellent service, also offered an outstanding range of services on board its S.E. 210s. This picture from a contemporaneous brochure produced by the airline, which went bankrupt in 2001, shows what was included. *Courtesy of Ron Handgraaf*

FRESH DESIGN FOR A NEW AIRLINER

After Air France, SAS and Swissair, the Finnish state airline Aero OY, which has been operating as Finnair since 1960, joined the circle of Caravelle customers. Like its Nordic neighbor, Finnair not only put its first jet into service with the S.E. 210 but also celebrated this event, which was so important for the company's history, with a series of design concepts that were intended to make flying with the Caravelle even more pleasant. Finnair entrusted the design of its S.E. 210 cabins to the renowned Finnish industrial and interior designer Ilmari Tapiovaara (1914–1999), who had learned his trade from the world-famous design icons of the twentieth century, including Alvar Aalto in London and Le Corbusier in Paris, among others. The Finnish designer Tapia Wirkkala, on the other hand, was responsible for the design of the onboard tableware specially developed for the Caravelle. With the exception of the stainless-steel Cumulus cutlery, the entire set was made of lightweight, reusable plastic. While SAS promoted its onboard culinary service in the form of a recipe booklet for re-creating its dishes, the manufacturer of the Finnair onboard tableware, Strömfors, offered it for sale to the general public until 1972. The set of six pieces was appropriately named Caravelle and was advertised with a picture of a Finnair machine of this type in the sales brochure. The very elegant onboard tableware took design cues from the lines of the S.E. 210 in many areas—such as the ashtray, reminiscent of the teardrop shape of the windows, and the handles of the coffee cup in the shape of the tail unit.

HELSINKI — HAMBURG

Petit Déjeuner

Aamiainen — Frukost

Jus de fruits
Hedelmämehu — Fruktsaft

Petit pain · Beurre
Leipä · Voi — Bröd · Smör

Confiture · Fromage
Marmeladi · Juusto — Marmelad · Ost

Plat chaud
Lämminruoka — Varmrätt

Café, Thé

HAMBURG — AMSTERDAM

Café, Thé

AMSTERDAM — LONDON/PARIS

Déjeuner Froid

Kylmä lounas — Kall lunch

Plat froid
Kylmä leikkelelautanen — Kall smörgåsassiett

Pâtisserie
Jälkiruokaleivos — Bakverk

Café, Thé

LONDON/PARIS — AMSTERDAM

Déjeuner Froid

Kylmä lounas — Kall lunch

Plat froid
Kylmä leikkelelautanen — Kall smörgåsassiett

Pâtisserie
Jälkiruokaleivos — Bakverk

Café, Thé

AMSTERDAM — HAMBURG

Cocktail

HAMBURG — HELSINKI

Diner

Päivällinen — Middag

Potage du jour
Keitto — Soppa

Plat chaud
Lämminruoka — Varmrätt

Salade de saison
Tuoresalaatti — Grönsallad

Fromage
Juusto — Ost

Café, Thé

Boissons

Champagne · Vins blancs · Vins rouges
Vermouth · Sherry · Manhattan · Martini
Gin · Liqueurs · Whisky · Cognac
Bière · Eaux Minérales

Finnair's menu was also visually very appealing, with dishes served on board their Caravelle between Helsinki and Paris, or London. *Courtesy of Finnish Aviation Museum*

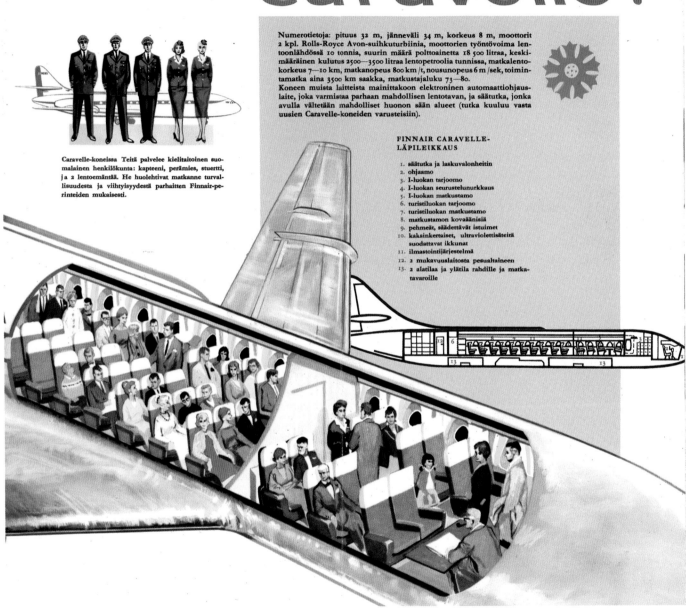

tämä on FINNAIR caravelle :

Caravelle-koneissa Teitä palvelee kielitaitoinen suomalainen henkilökunta: kapteeni, perämies, stuertti, ja 2 lentoemäntää. He huolehtivat matkanne turvallisuudesta ja viihtyisyydestä parhaiten Finnair-perinteiden mukaisesti.

Numerotietoja: pituus 32 m, jänneväli 34 m, korkeus 8 m, moottorit 2 kpl. Rolls-Royce Avon-suihkuturbiinia, moottorien työntövoima lentoonlähdössä 10 tonnia, suurin määrä polttoainetta 18 500 litraa, keskimääräinen kulutus 2500—3500 litraa lentopetroolia tunnissa, matkalentokorkeus 7—10 km, matkanopeus 800 km/t, nousunopeus 6 m/sek, toimintamatka aina 3500 km saakka, matkustajaluku 73—80.
Koneen muista laitteista mainittakoon elektroninen automaattiohjauslaite, joka varmistaa parhaan mahdollisen lentotavan, ja säätutka, jonka avulla vältetään mahdolliset huonon sään alueet (tutka kuuluu vasta uusien Caravelle-koneiden varusteisiin).

FINNAIR CARAVELLE-
LÄPILEIKKAUS

1. säätutka ja laskuvalonheitin
2. ohjaamo
3. I-luokan tarjoomo
4. I-luokan seurustelunurkkaus
5. I-luokan matkustamo
6. turistiluokan tarjoomo
7. turistiluokan matkustamo
8. matkustamon kovaäänisiä
9. pehmeät, säädettävät istuimet
10. kaksinkertaiset, ultraviolettisäteitä suodattavat ikkunat
11. ilmastointijärjestelmä
12. 2 mukavuuslaitosta pesualtaineen
13. 2 alatilaa ja ylätila rahdille ja matkatavaroille

This contemporaneous Finnair advertisement shows the layouts of the first- and tourist-class cabins on board the Caravelle. *Courtesy of Finnish Aviation Museum*

THE "CARAVELLE SAMBA"

In the late 1950s, Caravelle fever was rampant in northern Europe. Alongside the recipe book and the tableware available in the shops, Caravelle restaurants sprouted like mushrooms at the major airports. However, the climax of this unbridled enthusiasm for the S.E. 210 was the song "Caravelle Samba," specially commissioned by SAS for this aircraft type. "Voiçi la Caravelle . . . , here is the Caravelle . . ." intoned the Cliff Adams Singers together with the Hermanos Deniz Orchestra in 1959, at the beginning of the song pressed on vinyl. The single record, which could be played on only one side, was printed with an SAS Caravelle advertising photo on the front, while the lyrics, printed on the back, raved about the advantages of the Caravelle. It read: "There's music in the air . . . the melody of our modern times . . . the humming of SAS Caravelle pure jets sweeping the skies far overhead . . . saving time of all who travel in this swift jetliner to the many cities of the SAS jet network. Soft music is spread through the quietest airliner cabin in the world. And this is only one feature of the unique Scandinavian hospitality extended far above the clouds." As a special feature, the round panel first had to be pressed out of a plastic frame that had the typical teardrop shape of a Caravelle cabin window.

It was also popular in the early years of the jet age to advertise for airlines with songs. Sammy Davis Jr., for example, asked "Is the going great?" on behalf of Pan American Airways, and the group the 5th Dimension lyrically transformed their song "Up, Up and Away" into an advertising message for Trans World Airlines (TWA), to name just two examples. But an advertising song for just one aircraft type in the fleet—this is probably unique in civil aviation.

In 1959, to mark the launch of its first S.E. 210, SAS had the song Caravelle Samba composed, recorded by the Cliff Adams Singers, and pressed onto a record shaped like one of the Caravelle's windows. Of course, this record was also round so that it could be played, but it had to be pressed out of a teardrop-shaped frame. *Courtesy of Thomas Rosenqvist*

"THERE IS NO ONE HERE"

Many myths and facts surround the Caravelle, of which SAS compiled the most curious from its fifteen years of service with the Scandinavians on the occasion of its farewell to this aircraft type in 1974. The S.E. 210 was not only an aviation story, but also a relationship story in at least two cases. In 1959, Frenchman Jacques Declerq accompanied the first aircraft destined for SAS on the ferry flight from Toulouse to Stockholm as a Sud-Aviation technician. There he was to ensure for a while that the introduction of the aircraft into scheduled service went off without a hitch. What his employer did not expect—he fell in love with an SAS employee and stayed in Sweden! Conversely, Bengt Rehn, a Swede from the SAS technical department, was sent to Toulouse in the late 1950s to inspect the new French technical miracle—and stayed there after falling in love with the secretary of the head of Sud-Aviation and later marrying her. However, Rehn also remained loyal to SAS and was their technical representative in Toulouse even in the later Airbus days, when the Scandinavians ordered four A300B2s.

The royal families of the three SAS countries Denmark, Norway, and Sweden are still regular guests of SAS. And so one day, the then Danish queen Ingrid also flew on an SAS Caravelle. The purser offered the monarch, who was known to be a heavy smoker, a cigarette, but what happened next was a good example of Murphy's law: "Anything that can go wrong will go wrong." Because when Queen Ingrid pulled the ashtray out of the armrest, countless cigarette butts rained down on her. The cleaning staff had cleaned the whole plane down to the last corner for the royal passenger—except for this one ashtray!

If you wanted to recognize an SAS Caravelle pilot in the fifteen years of service of this jet, you had to turn his tie around. On the back of the tie, well hidden from prying eyes, was the distinctive sign of the "Caramel Club" of the Scandinavian S.E. 210 pilot corps. The drawing of a tiger in urgent need of the toilet was the external feature of this "esprit de corps." The members of the "Caramel Club" met for annual meetings and even published their own members' newsletter.

The Danish SAS flight captain Hans Fugl-Svendsen had a particularly nice anecdote to tell on the occasion of the Caravelle's decommissioning. The aircraft Finn Viking, with the registration OY-KRC, was on the Cairo–Khartoum leg on the occasion of the first flight of this route, when the crew routinely tried to make contact with their alternate airport, Wadi Haifa. But as hard as they tried, the radio remained silent at first. Only after a while did a hesitant voice come out of the ether and announce, "There is no one here."

After a training flight, SAS pilots enjoy a siesta in Abadan, Iran, in May 1959. These flights were carried out to gain experience on the new route from Copenhagen to Tehran. *Courtesy of SAS Museum*

A SAS Caravelle on the apron of Beirut airport. The bustling Lebanese capital, then known as the "Paris of the Middle East," was a lucrative stopover for many airlines on their way between Europe, Africa, and Asia. *SAS Museum*

FIRST COME, FIRST SERVED

In the 1960s, the logistics of catering (i.e., supplying passengers with special onboard tableware, drinks and meals) were not as sophisticated as they are today, especially with charter airlines. At the German LTU, for example, the cabin chiefs had to personally gather all the catering material needed for a particular flight in a storage room reserved for this purpose on the airport grounds before departure. Ute Bruns flew as a purser with LTU from 1966 to 2004, including on the Caravelle. She recalled in an interview recorded on the occasion of the airline's fiftieth anniversary in 2005 that each cabin chief rolled through this storage room with a large cart, like a luggage trolley at a railway station, and used it to assemble the catering material for the number of passengers booked on his next flight. With a bit of luck, one could still get some of every single item needed, such as glasses, cutlery, or salt and pepper packets, for good onboard service on the way from Germany to the holiday destinations around the Mediterranean. But the thrifty airline did not always order enough of every item—and so it was quite possible that there was no coffeepot or not enough cutlery in stock for the passengers. Not only in such cases was improvisation the order of the day at LTU.

It was a policy of LTU's management not to choose aircraft types that were flown by the competition. The Boeing models flown by Condor were therefore ruled out, as were the BAC-111s of Germanair and Bavaria. So they fell back on the Caravelle, which proved to be an excellent choice for the renowned German holiday airline. *Author's collection*

COPENHAGEN: THE CARAVELLE HUB

One year after the first scheduled flight by an SAS S.E. 210 Caravelle and at the same time as the delivery of the first Scandinavian Douglas DC-8-32 long-haul jets, Copenhagen Airport began the dawning jet age with a new "jet gateway" terminal. The Danish capital's airport is traditionally the major SAS hub and was also the starting point for most routes of this type to Africa, the Iberian Peninsula, and the Middle East in the dawning Caravelle era. In addition, the Danish charter airline Sterling had its base here and stationed its considerable Caravelle fleet, consisting of a total of thirty-four aircraft, at Copenhagen. In addition to the typical holiday destinations around the Mediterranean, the Sterling S.E. 210 route network, with refueling stops, extended as far as the Far East and North America. Together with the SAS aircraft, around fifty S.E. 210s were stationed there at times—more than at any other airport in the world.

When today's Terminal 2 was opened by Danish king Frederik on April 30, 1960, a row of shops, showers, and a hotel in the transit area offered all the travel comforts that are taken for granted today but were still sensational at the time. For the first time, passengers in Copenhagen could reach their aircraft with dry feet even in the rain via a pier system, which was still an absolute rarity, at least in Europe. As an anecdote, it should be noted here that these piers were not allowed to be wider than their platforms at the stations, at the insistence of the Danish state railways, so as not to give air traffic an additional competitive advantage. Fortunately, the jets did not have to fly as slowly as the trains ran! However, this did not stop the boom in air traffic, and only nine years later it was necessary to expand the handling facilities to include a domestic and arrival terminal as well as the third pier for handling the first jumbo jets. This basic layout of Copenhagen Airport, which has been expanded and modernized again and again, has been preserved in its form to this day, and the passenger piers, which now number six, have also met generous international standards for many years—entirely without the approval of the railways.

Copenhagen Airport had a new terminal built especially for the jet age that began with the Caravelle in 1959—now the airport's Terminal 2. *Courtesy of SAS Museum*

A Caravelle at the gate of Copenhagen's Kastrup Airport. It was not only the shapes of the French jetliner that were elegant, because at that time, flying was still something special, and people dressed accordingly. *Courtesy of SAS Museum*

AHEAD OF ITS TIME

According to a contemporaneous newspaper report (written by an M.Z. [Mitteldeutsche Zeitung] newspaper journalist, whose name was abbreviated F.O.B.), the following scene actually took place during a state visit made by an SAS Caravelle while still on the airport apron of the country visited:

Immediately after landing, reporters stormed the plane, pushed the stewardess aside, and stood in front of the foreign minister: "How do you like our country?" The minister, surprised by the hasty question, replied, "It is a beautiful country. When I was a child, I dreamt of being allowed to visit your country one day. Now, as a grown man and a member of the government, I will set foot on the soil of your country for the first time." . . . A reporter asked, "Will you be meeting our prime minister?" The minister stretched. "It will be a meeting," he said with emotion, "that will make history. I am also pleased to bring greetings from our country to His Majesty your King!" The minister stared into the suddenly frozen faces of the reporters. Finally, one of them remarked, "We have been a republic for forty years." Seeking help, the minister looked around. His personal advisor whispered something into his ear. Then the minister said: "Gentlemen, these modern jet planes—I thought we were still in Scandinavia."

In 1968, SAS changed its look, which can be seen on these two S.E. 210s in direct comparison. The original idea of the stylized Viking ship was retained, but the symbols used were abstracted and the color scheme more striking. *Courtesy of Tom Weihe*

CHAPTER 9
CARAVELLE PROGRAM MILESTONES

TAKEOFF INTO THE JET AGE

August 27, 1939: Maiden flight by the Heinkel He 178 V1, the world's first aircraft to fly with jet propulsion

April 6, 1948: The Vickers 618 Nene Viking experimental aircraft made the first flight by a pure jet airliner from London Heathrow to Paris-Villacoublay, carrying twenty-four passengers.

July 27, 1949: The only prototype of the AVRO Canada C-102 Jetliner to be completed made its first flight. The prototype was designed to carry thirty-six passengers. The type did not enter production, because production capacities in Canada and the United States were required to build fighter aircraft for the Korean War.

May 2, 1952: A Comet airliner of the British airline BOAC took off on the first scheduled jet airline flight in aviation history.

April 8, 1954: After the second crash of a Comet in four months, the type's airworthiness certificate was withdrawn. The first chapter in the story of commercial jet travel ended after less than two years.

An impressive size comparison between a Boeing 747-200 and a Caravelle III, taken in an SAS maintenance hangar in the early 1970s. *Courtesy of SAS Museum*

CARAVELLE TIMELINE

Date	Description
October 12, 1951	The French government and airline body Comité du Matériel Civil declare themselves in favor of the national short-and-medium-range jet project.
March 28, 1952	From the original twenty designs submitted, three are selected as the most promising candidates: the four-engine SNCASO S.O.60, the twin-engine Hurel-Dubois project, and the three-engine SNCASE X-210. After Rolls-Royce offered a more powerful version of the Avon, SNCASE was asked to convert the three-engine X-210 into a twin-engine design, resulting in the Caravelle.
July 1952	After initially proposing a three-engine aircraft with French SNECMA Atar E3 engines, Sud-Est, at the request of the selection committee, submits a twin-engine X-210 version with higher-thrust Rolls-Royce R.A. 16 Avon engines to the French Secretariat for Civil Aviation (SGACC) for evaluation.
September 1952	The Société Nationale de Construction Aéronautique du Sud-Est Aviation (SNCASE), Sud-Est Aviation for short, is awarded the contract.
January 3, 1953	A contract is signed for the construction of two flying prototypes as well as one fuselage each for material fatigue tests in the water tank and for static tests. The costs are borne by the French state.
July 6, 1953	Final confirmation of the order by the SGACC. Even before this date, the project lost its X (experimental) status and was henceforth officially called the S.E. 210.
September 1953	The Société Nationale de Construction Aéronautique du Sud-Est Aviation (SNCASE), or Sud-Est Aviation for short, is awarded the contract to build the French medium-range jet.
April 21, 1955	Official rollout of the first prototype at Toulouse
May 18, 1955	First taxiing trials
May 27, 1955	First flight by the Caravelle prototype F-WHHH / -BHHH
February 3, 1956	Air France, the French national airline, becomes the first customer for the S.E. 210, ordering twelve aircraft (plus twelve options).
May 6, 1956	First flight by the second Caravelle prototype F-WHHI / -BHHI

Date	Description
April 18, 1957	Two years before the Caravelle receives certification, Sud Aviation sends the second prototype, F-BHHI, on a sales tour through North and South America. It covers 29,734 miles (47,852 kilometers) in sixty-nine days and thirty-four stages.
April 2, 1958	The S.E. 210 receives its French type certification.
April 8, 1958	The American FAA certifies the type.
May 18, 1958	First flight by the Caravelle I production aircraft
February 28, 1959	The second S.E. 210 prototype, which has been rented for a month by SAS, arrives at Stockholm-Bromma for pilot training.
April 26, 1959	The Caravelle I Finn Viking takes off from Copenhagen on its maiden flight to Beirut. SAS thus becomes the first airline worldwide to operate the Caravelle in scheduled service.
May 6, 1959	Air France becomes the second airline to place the Caravelle in service, on the Paris–Orly–Istanbul route.
October 11, 1959	A VARIG Caravelle makes a record-breaking glide. From an altitude of 39,370 feet (12,000 meters), the aircraft flies 203 miles (327 kilometers) in forty minutes with its engines at idle.
December 12, 1959	The Brazilian carrier VARIG opens the "Caravelle Age" in South America with its first flight from Porto Alegre to New York.
February 10, 1960	Sud-Aviation and the US aircraft manufacturer Douglas Aircraft Company sign a far-reaching co-operation agreement. Douglas was responsible for sales and technical support for all customers, with the exception of airlines based in Europe and French-speaking regions around the globe. If the monthly Caravelle production rate of eight aircraft was exceeded, a second final-assembly line was to be set up at Douglas's Long Beach plant in California.
February 25, 1960	United Airlines orders twenty Caravelle VI-Rs (plus twenty options), the first version of the S.E. 210 to have thrust reversers. This remains the only order from a North American customer for new aircraft to be received.

Date	Description
September 7, 1960	Trans World Airlines Inc. (TWA) becomes the second US airline to order twenty aircraft (plus fifteen options)—this time of the Caravelle 10A version. They were to be equipped with General Electric CJ805-23C fan engines, based on the engines used by the Convair CV 990 Coronado. Two years later TWA canceled the order for economic reasons.
September 10, 1960	Maiden flight of VI-N version, with Rolls-Royce Avon engines but without thrust reversers. Fifty-three examples of this version were built.
December 29, 1960	Maiden flight of the Caravelle III, construction number 42, retrofitted with General Electric CJ805-23C "aft fan" engines, now designated Caravelle VII and serving as a flying test bed for Sud-Aviation and Douglas for the projected but unrealized Caravelle 10A.
February 6, 1961	The Caravelle VI-R—the first version of the S.E. 210 with thrust reversers, and the last with Avon engines—takes off for its first flight. The first customer is United Airlines.
May 31, 1961	United Airlines takes delivery of the first Caravelle VI-R, N1001U, Ville de Toulouse (City of Toulouse). All United aircraft are named after French cities, starting with the production location of the S.E. 210.
March 3, 1964	Maiden flight of the Caravelle 10B3 "Super B" or "Super Caravelle," with Pratt & Whitney JT8D-1 and -7 engines. Twenty-two were built—ten of them for launch customer Finnair.

Date	Description
January 18, 1965	The first Caravelle 10R, destined for launch customer Royal Jordanian Airlines, goes into service. It is one of twenty examples produced of this S.E. 210 variant, powered by Pratt & Whitney JT8D-1 and -7.
April 21, 1967	Maiden flight of the combi version Caravelle 11R, equipped with a large side cargo door. Just six examples of this version, developed for Air Afrique, were completed.
December 28, 1968	The S.E. 210 is the first passenger jet to be certified for Category III landings (horizontal visibility: 492 feet [150 meters]; decision height: 49.2 feet [15 meters]).
January 9, 1969	A Caravelle of the French domestic airline Air Inter completes the first CAT III landing on a scheduled-passenger flight.
May 18, 1971	The Danish charter airline Sterling Airways is the first customer to take delivery of the first example of the final version, the Caravelle 12, with a maximum capacity of 140 passengers. Just twelve aircraft of this largest version of the Caravelle were built. Originally registered in Denmark as OY-SAC, the first aircraft flew with the French domestic airline Air Inter from October 1980 until its retirement in March 1991, with the registration F-BNOH.
March 8, 1973	Production of the type S.E. 210 comes to an end after two completed prototypes and 280 series aircraft delivered.

Danish Sterling Airways tried to gain a foothold in the Asian charter market with the Philippine airline Transasian. However, the local authorities refused to approve the new airline, and so it got no further than two VI-Rs painted in Transasian colors. RP-C970, which had previously flown with United, was photographed in Copenhagen on May 7, 1976, shortly after its return from the Philippines. *Courtesy of Tom Weihe*

CHAPTER 10
SPECIFICATIONS: ALL S.E. 210 VARIANTS IN DETAIL

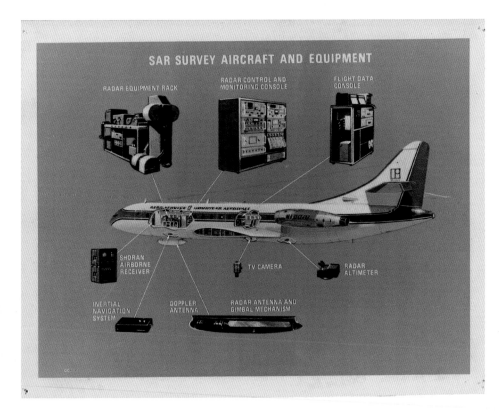

The overview of Caravelle variants is divided into the tables shown on pages 136 and 137, one for versions I to VI, powered by Rolls-Royce Avon engines, and one for the Caravelle 10 to 12, with Pratt & Whitney JT8D engines. Particular importance was attached to the accuracy of the data. Therefore, only original historical documents from Caravelle customers as well as from Sud-Aviation served as the basis for the creation of the data.

ROLLS-ROYCE-POWERED VERSIONS OF THE S.E. 210 CARAVELLE I TO VI-R

	Caravelle I*	Caravelle III	Caravelle VI-N	Caravelle VI-R
Dimensions				
Wingspan	112 ft., 6 in.	112 ft., 6 in.	112 ft., 6 in.	112 ft., 6 in.
Overall length	105 ft.	105 ft.	105 ft.	105 ft.
Overall height	28 ft., 6 in.	28 ft., 6 in.	28 ft., 6 in.	28 ft., 6 in.
Wing area (ft.²)	1,579	1,579	1,579	1,579
Power plants				
Type	R.R. Avon RA.29/1 Mk. 522	R.R. Avon RA.29/3 Mk. 527	R.R. Avon RA.29/6 Mk. 531**	R.R. Avon RA.29/6 Mk. 533R***
Max. takeoff thrust (lbs.)	10,500	11,400	12,200	12,600
Fuel capacity (US gal.)	5,020	5,020	5,020	5,020
Weights				
Max. takeoff weight (lbs.)	95,900	101,413	105,800	110,230
Max. landing weight (lbs.)	91,430	96,560	100,750	104,990
Performance				
Max. speed (mph)	467	498	525	525
Corresponding altitude (ft.)	24,600	25,250	25,900	24,950
Cruising speed (mph)	460	493	506	506
Corresponding altitude (ft.)	30,000	30,000	32,800	32,900
at average weight of (lbs.)	86,000	88,000	90,000	92,500
Max. payload (lbs.)	18,454	18,520	17,415	18,080
Range with max. payload (nm)	810	915	1,270	1,240
Takeoff distance (ft.)	5,900	5,900	6,365	6,725
Landing distance (ft.)	5,775	6,000	6,100	5,315
Capacities				
Max. passengers	99	99	99	99
Cargo/baggage useful volume:				
Cabin (ft.³)	212	212	212	212
Under cabin floor (ft.³) 282	282	282	282	

Sources: SAS, Sud-Aviation
* Caravelle I/Ia were upgraded to Caravelle III standard
** Alternative version Mk. 532
*** Alternative version Mk. 532R

PRATT & WHITNEY-POWERED VERSIONS OF THE S.E. 210 CARAVELLE 10B TO 12

	Caravelle 10B	Caravelle 10B3	Caravelle 11R	Caravelle 10R	Caravelle 12
Dimensions					
Wingspan	112 ft., 6 in.	112 ft., 6 in.	112 ft., 6 in.	112 ft., 6 in.	112 ft., 6 in.
Overall length	105 ft.	108 ft., 3 in.	105 ft.	105 ft.	118 ft., 9 in.
Overall height	28 ft., 6 in.	28 ft., 6 in.	28 ft., 6 in.	28 ft., 6 in.	29 ft., 7 in.
Wing area (ft.²)	1,579	1,579	1,579	1,579	1,579
Power plants					
Type*	P&W JT8D-7*	P&W JT8D-7	P&W JT8D-7	P&W JT8D-7	P&W JT8D-9
Max. takeoff thrust (lbs.)	14,000	14,000	14,000	14,000	14,500
Fuel capacity (US gal.)	5,020	5,020	5,020	5,020	5,020
Weights					
Max. takeoff weight (lbs.)	114,606	123,450	114,606	114,606	127,860
Max. landing weight (lbs.)	109,130	109,130	109,130	109,130	109,130
Performance					
Cruising speed (mph)	498	498	498	498	510
Corresponding altitude (ft.)	25,000	25,000	25,000	25,000	25,000
Max. payload (lbs.)	20,720	20,056	19,890	20,720	29.100
Range with max. payload (nm)	1,565	1,435	1,511	1,565	1,370
Capacities					
Max. passengers	99	104	99	Combi max. 99 passengers, plus 6 pallets of freight	140

Sources: Sud-Aviation
* Some aircraft upgraded from Pratt & Whitney JT8D-1

Aero Service Corporation, once based in Houston, Texas, used the Caravelle VI-R purchased from United Airlines for aerial mapping. For this purpose, the former Ville de Toulouse N1001U was equipped with a radar system called "Synthetic Aperture Radar" for contour detection, which was highly advanced for its time. This aircraft provided graphic coverage of all of Brazil, parts of Indonesia and the Philippines, Liberia, Gabon, and Japan, as well as large areas of the US and other countries. After the company's bankruptcy in August 1990, the historically significant N1001U was transferred to the Pima Air and Space Museum in Tucson, Arizona. *Courtesy of Pima Air and Space Museum*

CHAPTER 11
COMPETING JETLINERS

Delta Air Lines was a loyal customer for Boeing jets for many years, and not only the 737-200. *Author's collection*

BOEING 737

When Boeing began project studies for a small twin-engine jet on May 8, 1964, the competition had long since positioned itself in the market with its own designs. In addition to the Caravelle, British Aircraft Corporation presented its BAC-111 in 1961, while archrival Douglas in Long Beach, California, presented its 2086 model in the same year, which gave rise to the DC-9, officially launched in April 1963. The concept initially pursued by Boeing followed the designs of the other producers and envisaged a small jet with a narrow fuselage and two engines in the tail. For a long time, Boeing discussed the design of the 737 internally. Finally, several basic arguments tipped the scales in favor of the familiar 737 configuration. First, weight could be saved by placing the engines under the wings, since a larger T tail requires a heavier tail structure. The Boeing engineers used this saved weight to use the heavier but more powerful Pratt & Whitney JT8D engine. In addition, the reduced empty weight made it possible to use the 727 cabin cross section, and thus the transport of more passengers in an aircraft of the same size. The way was paved for the homogeneous Boeing 707/720/727/737 aircraft family.

BOEING 727

In May 1958—five months before the first 707 entered service with Pan Am—Boeing president William "Bill" Allen appointed his talented engineer John E. "Jack" Steiner to head a planning group for the development of a new short-and-medium-range jet. He worked closely with Maynard Pennell, who had already made a name for himself designing Boeing's B-29 and 707. When Steiner took over the project management of the new aircraft type, there was not much more than a type designation: 7 2 7. Even after examining thirty-eight different design variants of the jet, which at that time was still a twin-engine concept, Steiner and Pennell were dissatisfied with the results. Developing a small, economical jet seemed to them almost an impossibility. While Steiner and Pennell were not convinced by any of their twin-engine designs—let alone a four-engine jet—a telephone conversation between Jack Steiner and Robert W. "Bob" Rummel, head of the TWA engineering department and personal advisor to TWA owner Howard Hughes, brought the breakthrough. Half serious, half in jest, Rummel suggested building a three-engine jet as a compromise. The more intensively Steiner and Pennell examined this idea, the more it seemed to them both a curse and a blessing. On the one hand, a third engine made it possible to achieve the planned maximum takeoff weight; on the other hand, the design of a three-engine jet initially raised more questions than it provided answers. Where should the third engine be placed in the tail? How should the wings and tail look from an aerodynamic point of view? And what type of engine was to power the jet? The number of technological question marks was so great that Steiner and Pennell initially shelved the three-engine jet and turned their attention once again to the concept of a four-engine jet. Together with Boeing chief aerodynamicist Joe Sutter, the team of Steiner and Pennell finally set about a conceptual reboot and put aside all previous plans. The result of countless new designs and 5,400 hours of testing in the wind tunnel was wings with a high-lift system consisting of slats and three-part flaps that minimized takeoff and landing speeds, and thus also the takeoff and landing distances

required for the 727. High- and low-speed ailerons enabled the 727 to be controlled safely in all speed ranges, while spoilers on the upper surface of the wings, effective main gear brakes, and thrust reversers on the three Pratt & Whitney JT8D turbofan engines chosen for propulsion reduced the rollout distance. Eddie Rickenbacker, CEO of Eastern Air Lines, urged Boeing to install a retractable tail stair to reduce turnaround times.

The Boeing 727 was offered to airlines from the summer of 1960 at a unit price of US$4.2 million. However, the profit potential of the airlines was so great, thanks to the uncompromisingly economical 727 design, that the airlines themselves accepted this price, which was very high by the standards of the time. One of the reasons for the enthusiasm of potential customers was the new type's extremely short takeoff and landing distances. And this was one of the core requirements, especially of those US airlines that had Chicago Midway Airport; Washington, DC, National Airport; or New York La Guardia, with their short runways on their flight schedules. After certification of the aircraft type, the launch customer Eastern Air Lines was able to ceremoniously take delivery of its first jet on October 29, 1963—one of 1,832 Boeing 727s built by September 18, 1984.

Instead of honoring the signed purchase contract for twenty examples of the S.E. 210 10A "La Nouvelle Caravelle," TWA canceled the order and shortly afterward acquired Boeing 727 aircraft. *Courtesy of Jon Proctor*

DOUGLAS DC-9

Although the DC-9 temporarily became the most built jetliner, only to relinquish this title to the Boeing 737, its prospects did not look very promising at the time of the program's launch in April 1963. It was only a month after the go-ahead that Delta Air Lines placed a meager first order for fifteen aircraft. Much to the manufacturer's relief, however, sales figures picked up strongly shortly afterward. The prototype's maiden flight on February 25, 1965, was followed by an intensive flight test program before the first DC-9-14-series aircraft entered service with Delta Air Lines on December 8, 1965. Within a few months, Continental, Eastern, and TWA also received their first aircraft, introducing jet comfort even on less frequented routes. As popular as this first DC-9 variant was at first, the launch customers quickly parted with their DC-9-10s as soon as larger versions with lower operating costs became available. The DC-9-21 and -41 series were special versions, developed especially for SAS, replacing the Flying Vikings' Caravelles by 1974. Swissair was the first customer for the DC-9-51, the last version marketed exclusively as the "DC-9," before McDonnell Douglas took another major step in the evolution of the DC-9 basic type with the aircraft families known as the MD-80, MD-95, and MD-90-30.

SAS eschewed the more advanced Caravelle versions with Pratt & Whitney JT8D engines and opted for the DC-9 family of aircraft as an alternative, which included the DC-9-21, built especially for SAS. *Courtesy of SAS*

BIBLIOGRAPHY

As if time had stopped for a moment, the Panair do Brasil Caravelle from the first chapter has moved just a little farther while you were reading this book. *Courtesy of Ministério da Defesa / Comando da Aeronáutica / Museu Aeroespacial, Rio de Janeiro*

Baumgartner, Peter. *Ein Lächeln fliegt um die Welt, Eine Zeitreise durch die Geschichte von Austrian Airlines.* Vienna: Metroverlag, Austrian Airlines Corporate Communications, 2017.

Bergman, Bill, and S. Artur Svensson. *Ett år i luften: Flygets årsbok, 1959–1960.* Malmö, Sweden: Allhems Förlag, 1959.

Bjurtoft, Marianne, Birgit Dahlberg, Gunilla Emthén, and Gunnel Högling. *Dröm och verklighet: Ett yrke i det blå.* Stockholm: Freddy Stenboms Förlag AB, 2006.

Contemporaneous documents, Scandinavian Airlines.

Contemporaneous documents, Swissair.

Contemporaneous documents, VARIG.

Davies, R. E. G. *Pan Am: An Airline and Its Aircraft.* Twickenham, UK: Hamlyn, 1987.

Eastwood, A. B., and J. R. Roach. *Jet Airliner Production List.* West Drayton, UK: Aviation Hobby Shop, 1989.

Flores, Jackson, Jr. *VARIG: A Brazilian Star.* Rio de Janeiro, Argentina: Action Editora, 1997.

Gieselmann, Heiko, and Katina Treese. *LTU Rückblick—5 Jahrzehnte Lebensfreude.* Mühlheim an der Ruhr, Germany: Ok! Kommunikation, 2005.

Inside SAS: House Organ for SAS Personnel, October 1974. Stockholm: Scandinavian Airlines.

Monmarson-Frémont, Pascale, and Véronique Damas-Peyraud. *Caravelle, Willkommen an Bord einer Legende.* Bielefeld, Germany: Delius Klasing Verlag, 2008.

Rummel, Robert W. *Howard Hughes and TWA.* Washington, DC: Smithsonian Institution Press, 1991.

S.E. 210 CARAVELLE, Instruction Manual. 3 vols. Paris: Sud-Aviation, 1958–1964.

Von Vegesack, Alexander, and Jochen Eisenbrand. *Airworld: Design und Architektur für die Flugreise.* Weil am Rhein, Germany: Vitra Design Stiftung, 2004.

Waddington, Terry. *Great Airliners.* Vol. 4, *McDonnell Douglas DC-9.* Miami, FL: World Transport Press, 1998.

Wegg, John. "Caravelle Sunset." *Airliners: The World's Airline Magazine,* Winter 1991.

Yearbook. Stockholm: Scandinavian Airlines, 1967–1970 and 1974.

A Swissair SE 210 III on approach in 1969 to Basel-Mulhouse airport as flight SR 433 from Vienna, via Zurich to BSL. *Reto Fasciati collection, bsl-mlh-planes.net*

ACKNOWLEDGMENTS

Numerous individuals and organizations contributed to the success of this book. I would especially like to thank:

Xavier Aldair, Ministério da Defesa / Comando da Aeronáutica / Museu Aeroespacial, Brazil

Nils Alegren, owner of www.flyCaravelle.com, Germany / Sweden Alitalia Press Office, Italy

John Bezosky, collections manager, Pima Air and Space Museum, USA

Ron Handgraaf, ronsaviationshop, the Netherlands

Rolf Keller, www.bsl-mlh-planes.net, Switzerland

Bernd Keidel, Motorbuch Verlag, Germany

Matias Laitinen, head of collections, Finnish Aviation Museum

Rand Masa'deh, senior corporate communications supervisor, Corporate Communications Dept., Royal Jordanian Airlines

Dave Robinson, www.aviationancestry.co.uk, Great Britain

Thomas Rosenqvist, Sweden

Janne Salonen, chairman, Aviation Museum Society Finland

Vanessa Schmidt, assistant corporate communications & media relations, Austrian Airlines

Ralph Steffen, Claasen Communication GmbH, Germany

Tom Weihe and Musante Larsen, Nicolai, Denmark

And my beloved wife, Carol Oxberry, for her continued support, advice, and patience in the making of this book!

THE AUTHOR
WOLFGANG BORGMANN

Wolfgang Borgmann's enthusiasm for aviation was passed on to him by his parents, who were active in the aviation field. In his early years, he began building up an aviation historical collection that provides numerous rare photos and documents, as well as exciting background information, for his books. Since April 2000, Borgmann has been active as an author and, until February 2022, as a freelance aviation journalist. Since then he has worked as an editor for the leading German civil aviation magazine *Aero International*. He lives in Oerlinghausen, Germany. His website is www.aerojournalist.de.